PRAISE FOR
STOPPING THE ROAD

OTHER HISTORIES
BY JACK FISHER

STOPPING THE ROAD

THE CAMPAIGN AGAINST ANOTHER TRANS-SIERRA HIGHWAY

Cover designed by: Siori Kitajima, SFAppWorks LLC
www.sfappworks.com
Cover artwork by Peggy Schotz
Formatting by Siori Kitajima and Ovidiu Vlad, SFAppWorks LLC
eBook Formatted by Ovidiu Vlad

Cataloging-in-Publication data for this book is available from the
Library of Congress

ISBN-13: 978-0-9916629-3-7
ISBN-10: 0991662938

Published by The Sager Group LLC
www.TheSagerGroup.Net
info@TheSagerGroup.Net

STOPPING THE ROAD

THE CAMPAIGN AGAINST ANOTHER TRANS-SIERRA HIGHWAY

BY JACK FISHER

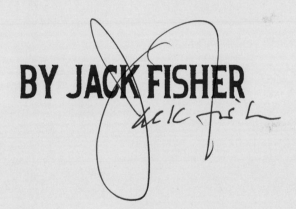

THE SAGER GROUP

Artifex Te Adiuva

Dedicated to
Norman B. "Ike" Livermore,
Packer, Conservationist,
Public Servant

"We shall base modern history... on the narratives of eyewitnesses, and on genuine and original documents."
—Leopold von Ranke, German historian, 1795–1886

TABLE OF CONTENTS

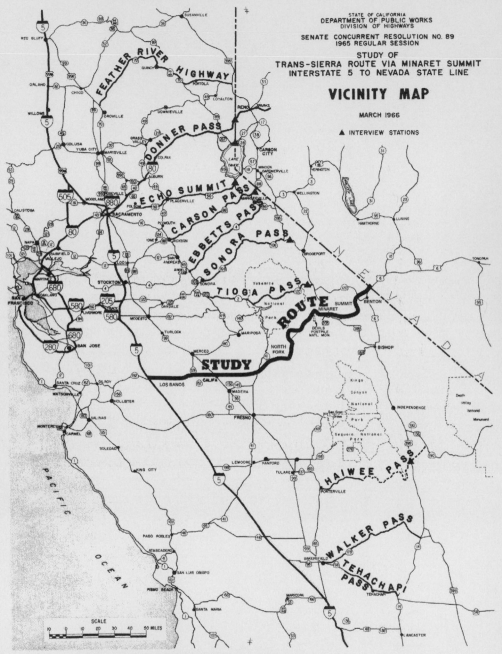

STATE OF CALIFORNIA
DEPARTMENT OF PUBLIC WORKS
DIVISION OF HIGHWAYS

SENATE CONCURRENT RESOLUTION NO. 89
1965 REGULAR SESSION

STUDY OF
TRANS-SIERRA ROUTE VIA MINARET SUMMIT
INTERSTATE 5 TO NEVADA STATE LINE

VICINITY MAP

MARCH 1966

▲ INTERVIEW STATIONS

SCALE
10 0 10 20 30 40 50 MILES

PROLOGUE

J UNE 2006 MARKED the fiftieth anniversary of federal legislation that guaranteed financing of America's omnipresent Interstate Highway System. Championed by President Eisenhower and supported by Republicans and Democrats alike, the Federal-Aid Highway Act of 1956 provided an unprecedented 9-to-1 funding match for state and local governments willing to ante the first 10 percent of construction costs. Over a span of five decades, 46,876 miles of limited access highways were placed in service. News accounts of this grand achievement often included a map showing a dense network of roads filling the nation's landscape... except for one conspicuous triangular gap reaching from central Utah westward across Nevada and California to the Pacific shore.[1]

Whereas Interstate 10 and I-40 to the south and I-80 and I-90 to the north extend from one coast to the other, I-70 out of Baltimore ends abruptly at its junction with I-15 south of Salt Lake City. The resulting breach has little to do with the failure of legislators in Utah, Nevada, and California to exploit the highway act's generous subsidy. The reality is that beyond its western terminus, I-70 had nowhere useful to go without an effective route across the Sierra Nevada.

Engineering wasn't the problem either. Precedents for high altitude road construction were long established; I-70 already crosses the Colorado Rockies and Utah's Wasatch Range, while I-80 transits both the Rockies in Wyoming and the Sierra Nevada at Donner Summit. The obstacle standing in the path of road builders was entirely political in nature. For as long as a motive had existed for constructing another highway across the Sierra Nevada, opponents saw only the loss of a sacred wilderness to commercial interests. Remarkably, organized resistance came from both wilderness advocates and Eastern Sierra businessmen who recognized little economic advantage to the road.[2]

Meanwhile, community leaders in Fresno and Madera Counties west of the Sierra imagined a boon to local commerce evolving from improved access to the nation's expanding transportation grid. California's major ocean ports lay to the north in Oakland, served by a railroad corridor and ready access to I-80, and to the south in San Pedro and Long Beach, where rail and highway networks abounded. Fresno's primary economy was based on an agricultural bounty from the surrounding Central Valley, nearly all of it requiring shipment 200 miles north or south before distribution to faraway markets. Neither Madera nor Fresno could hope to serve as a transport hub while standing before an uninterrupted mountain barrier.[3]

As of 1966, there were ten highways already traversing the Sierra Nevada, but none of them were closer to Fresno than 110 miles. Why not build another crossing? asked the road advocates. One prospect was the proposed addition of a particular forest road to the state highway plan, making possible eventual completion of another year-round thoroughfare on the scale of existing US 50 near Lake Tahoe. Forest Highway 100 (FH 100) had functioned since the 1920s for multiple uses, including timber harvest, fire control, and recreation access. Extending eastward from North Fork on the western slope as far as Clover Meadow, it became a hiking trail for fourteen more miles before it reached Reds Meadow Pack Station. Continuing as a drivable road past Devils Postpile National Monument, it climbing to Minaret Summit before joining CA 203 in Mammoth Lakes. This was a right-of-way with ample historical precedent, first as a popular trade route for natives and later as the "Old French Trail," used for pack trains bringing supplies to nineteenth century–gold prospectors in boomtown Mammoth City. Now as a proposed modern highway, its 9,000-foot mountain passes would pose a greater challenge for snow clearance than 7,200-foot Donner Summit. This singular geographic feature would haunt the road's prospect for decades.

"Not if we can stop it," was the announced position of vocal citizens of Mammoth Lakes, where the earliest phases of construction might someday begin. Year-round inhabitants and seasonal visitors to the Eastern Sierra community favored maintaining a pristine winter ski resort and unspoiled summer getaway. While a few business owners relished the prospect of increased traffic, most were horrified by the thought of a high-density commercial thoroughfare, especially one that might link with Interstate 70.

The battle was joined, and it continued for nearly a half century. Numerous skirmishes were fought on both sides of the Sierra. Reams of documentary evidence were generated. Advocates in favor and against the project testified at countless hearings. City and town councils, county boards of supervisors, and all of the respective chambers of commerce hurled charges and countercharges at one another for years running. In Sacramento as well as in Washington, DC, there was intense backroom dealing over a remote forest highway representing enterprise for some and desecration of nature to others.

Today we know the proposed road improvements were never completed, a modern trans-Sierra thoroughfare was not carved out of a forest sanctuary, and the imagined westward extension of I-70 was never given priority by interstate planning authorities. This book tells the story of a thoroughfare that was never completed, from its nineteenth century–origins to its twentieth century–disqualification as a state highway; from its potential to become a federally financed all-season transportation link to its 1972 downfall when California governor Ronald Reagan rode on horseback to a place in the Sierra Nevada where mule trains once passed and announced to an audience of packers, foresters, and out-of-place political journalists that the wilderness surrounding them would not be partitioned with concrete by order of President Richard Nixon. There followed an additional twelve-year campaign to secure the decision for all time by converting the longstanding right-of-way into a federally designated wilderness.

How did it happen? Why was an assembly of local citizens with one purpose in mind more effective in the long run than a ubiquitous national organization like the Sierra Club? Given a Republican in the White House and another serving as California's governor-neither one considered sensitive to environmental issues-how could a major thoroughfare promoted by powerful interests be decisively removed from impending action? For the final step, obliteration of the highway corridor, why did a Republican governor turn to a Democratic senator for help before enlisting support from a fellow Republican?

Such are the ironies and permutations inherent in the American political process, that when the existing record is examined and living participants are invited to recall their victory, a compelling tale is revealed.

ROADS RUNNING WILD

WRITING IN A 1938 issue of *American Forests* under the title, "Roads Running Wild," recent Stanford University graduate and mule packer Norman B. Livermore Jr. argued persuasively for limits on road building into the Sierra Nevada. He never forgot the shock of encountering an automobile close by the John Muir Trail while leading a pack trip in 1930.[4]

Ike, as known to friends and fellow packers, had camped at Pumice flat near Reds Meadow. While picking up supplies at the nearby pack station, he learned of a road just built by a mining company for truck access. With federal funding, it was extended to Devils Postpile National Monument and then on to the pack station. "Seeing automobiles in a wilderness was like a stab in the heart," he later recalled. When a packer predicted the road was sure to continue westward across the entire range some day, Livermore promised himself to use whatever power he might acquire to stop that road from going any farther. Forty-two years later, he would hold the necessary power and keep his pledge.[5]

Born to a prominent California family in 1911, Livermore's parents nurtured in him a facility with life outdoors. At Montesol, the family ranch near Calistoga, California, he learned to ride and care for horses. At sixteen, he rode his own horse two hundred miles from Ojai to Monterey, living close to the land like John Muir, whose books he carried with him. The following year, Livermore rode his motorcycle the length of the Sierra Nevada looking for work in the national forests, but government funds for summer employment were scarce in 1928. Only because he knew how to shoe a mule, he secured a job as packer's assistant, starting out as the trail cook's helper. The following year his responsibilities expanded, and he was soon leading private parties into the backcountry. Fellow packers marveled that a college boy could acquire the skills of their trade so quickly. In his trail diaries, Livermore recorded the names of the mules in addition to party members, believing pack stock were just as important as paying customers. Mentored by Mineral King Pack Station owner Phil Davis, he imagined committing his entire life to wilderness packing.[6]

Writing about his trail experiences years later, Livermore described two kinds of packer: first, "the old-salt cowpuncher who spoke a vernacular tongue and was unexcelled at handling stock," and second, "the pack train owner who is more focused on running a successful business." He learned from both but identified with the operators. Even as a university student, Livermore earned respect for backcountry savvy and his organizational skills.

A social science major at Stanford, he also took accounting courses at the urging of his father. Following graduation in 1933, Livermore attended Harvard Business School where his research project examined California's tourist packing business. Continuing graduate study at Stanford, he compiled data based on interviews and returned questionnaires, then submitted a thesis titled "The Tourist Packing Business in the High Sierra Region." Offered an opportunity to present his findings at a 1935 Commonwealth Club symposium, the newly minted MBA was both the youngest participant and the speaker with more facts than anyone else. Livermore began by defining wilderness as a region far enough removed from drivable roads to require packing in for a full day. Regarding backcountry visitors, he differentiated the "self-regulated man who enters the wilderness with a pack animal" from the "Coney Islander," meaning a tourist who behaves in the forest as he would in the city. "Somewhere in between is the 'autoist' whose aim is to get away

from the city but is too lazy to fully engage with his surroundings."
A reporter in the audience was impressed by Livermore's charac-
terizations and featured his presentation in the November 21, 1935,
San Francisco Chronicle.[7]

Livermore could identify only five million acres of primitive land remaining in California. He wanted them all protected
from road assault but gave priority to the 2.3 million uninterrupted acres that lay between Tioga Pass in Yosemite National Park and
Walker Pass south of Sequoia National Forest. He criticized the Civilian Conservation Corps preference for building roads instead of
mending trails. He cited the Boy Scout who wished to fulfill his
fourteen-mile hiking requirement inside a wilderness but could select from only seven areas in all of California.[8]

The Commonwealth Club, the nation's oldest and largest
public affairs forum, embraced Livermore's recommendations and
passed a resolution warning against further road building. A public statement read in part: "We believe that California's undeveloped high mountain areas have been reduced dangerously near to
a minimum for the welfare of the State, and that no further intru-
sions by the building of roads should be allowed without convincing proof of public necessity." The vote in committee was 7–2, and
by the membership 650–70, a remarkable demonstration of environmental advocacy considering the club was largely made up of
businessmen.

At the urging of Livermore, whose study also demonstrated that the packing industry's interests would be more effectively advanced as a collective organization, a group of packers met
in Porterville in 1935 to form the High Sierra Packer's Association.
Owens Valley packers tried without success to organize in 1928,
but Livermore later helped them establish the Eastside High Sierra Packer's Association. Soon after the two groups joined as a trade
organization, members qualified for tort litigation insurance.[9]

While visiting Porterville, Livermore learned about the proposed road across nearby Haiwee Pass to Lone Pine in the Eastern
Sierra. First promoted in 1933 as the Porterville-Lone Pine Recreational Highway and designated in 1935 for state funding, the
project required ninety miles of road improvement plus forty miles

of new construction over 10,500-foot Mulkey Pass. Like most trans-Sierra highway proposals, construction costs were underestimated at $800,000, with cost of maintenance and snow removal left out. The idea languished for years and faded for lack of economic interest.[10]

Mountains continued to attract Livermore's fascination wherever he went. As the star catcher for Stanford's baseball team, he earned a position on the 1936 US Olympic Team that drew the largest recorded audience to date for a baseball game-including Adolph Hitler. But the exhilaration of playing ball in Berlin could not compete with continuing his journey to India where he explored the trails, passes, and mountain camps of the Himalayan Range. Years later, Livermore recalled the price he paid: five dollars a day for five servants and four ponies to guide him through the highest passes of Ladakh.

After returning to the Mineral King Pack Outfit, Livermore led parties of his own throughout the Sierra. Pleasing clients meant arriving in camp first in order to stake out comfortable commissary and latrine areas before mule handlers claimed these for themselves. Among his responsibilities were the Annual Sierra Club Outings with pack trains of 100–120 head. In 1937, he packed in the largest group of his career requiring three hundred stock. With financial participation from his father, he purchased a fractional interest in a pack station and later acquired property in the Mineral King area.

The attack on Pearl Harbor ended Livermore's wilderness idyll. War also brought financial ruin to the Sierra packers, who watched in horror as business vanished almost overnight. Livermore tried for the army's Tenth Mountain Division, also the Office of Strategic Services but without success. Instead, he was commissioned a lieutenant junior grade for naval service at the Sicily, Palau, Iwo Jima, and Okinawa invasions. He rarely spoke of these experiences ever again. On furlough in 1943, he married Virginia "Dina" Pennoyer, "the girl I met while planning for a pack trip and never forgot."[11]

Returning to California and the Sierra Nevada in 1946, Livermore learned that pack outfits had sold much of their stock, retaining only enough horses and mules to outfit small Sierra Club outings. So he organized cooperative ventures with pooled stock. Despite modest success, nothing he attempted could revive business enough for a man with a family coming. Sale of his Mineral King interest permitted him to invest with partners in Mount Whitney Pack Trains, a gratifying supplement to his new career as an accountant. In 1952, with a family that included five children, he became treasurer of the Pacific Lumber Company, where he would remain until entering public service in 1968.

Ike Livermore leading pack train 1936
CREDIT: *David Livermore*

THROUGHOUT HIS LONG career, Livermore never lost his love for the wilderness of the High Sierra. A member of the Sierra Club since 1936, he rose to serve on its board of directors. Long years of backcountry service to members defused any potential concerns about a lumber company executive influencing the organization's policies. Livermore was, however, displeased with the Sierra Club's ambivalent posture on wilderness road development. Together with other conservation organizations, the Sierra Club had agreed with state authorities in 1938, offering a contradictory message: "If necessity called for one more Sierra crossing, best that it be in the vicinity of Mammoth Pass rather than at any other point." It was a position that Livermore could never support and worked tirelessly to reverse.

He understood why the Sierra Club chose not to fight the evolving highway over Tioga Pass; there had been some kind of road there since the 1880s when the Great Sierra Consolidated Silver Company first commissioned a wagon route from Calaveras County to Bennettville, now an abandoned mining site near Tioga Pass. The National Park Service (NPS) later assumed responsibility and improved the road repeatedly. An eastern approach to the pass through Lee Vining Canyon was first constructed in 1903. The road's 1961–1967 modernization included a rerouting that made it one of the most spectacular mountain highways in the nation.[12]

Livermore's attitude about more Sierra roads between Tioga and Walker Passes remained nonnegotiable. Most road programs, he believed, were initiated by local chambers of commerce, promoted by their respective political representatives, backed by highway authorities, and supported by agencies grateful for the expanded responsibility. He knew that established road interests were just as powerful in the 1950s as they were in the 1930s when he first took notice. Only the clearest demonstration of public resistance— pleading with legislators, organizing petitions, and initiating electoral propositions—could forestall a road network advancing into the wilderness. For 9,500-foot Minaret Summit near Mammoth Mountain, how could anyone think an all-season road could be built, he asked, when 9,941-foot Tioga Pass closed every winter?

Few remembered that the Southern Pacific Railroad had conducted a survey for construction of a highway over a pass near Mammoth Mountain as early as 1901. The railroads continued expanding their networks in America and kept searching for new routes. Railroad construction requires a parallel service road, but there is no evidence of road planning near Mammoth at that time. With establishment of the Devils Postpile National Monument in 1911, National Park Service interest in public access commenced. Mining interests built their road in 1929, a treacherous two-thousand-foot descent from Minaret Summit to the mines at Minaret

Creek. Government funding later allowed for its designation as FH 100 and its extension to the national monument and the pack station beyond.[13]

Long before popular efforts to preserve wilderness culminated in landmark legislation, selected portions of established national forests were designated primitive areas with stricter limits placed on timber harvest. In 1931, Secretary of Agriculture Arthur Hyde reduced the respective borders of the High Sierra and Mount Dana–Minarets primitive areas to create a five-mile gap between them for eventual road development. This federally designated corridor not only approximated the route surveyed by the railroad at the beginning of the century but also provided an opening for the aforementioned road. Nothing actionable in terms of highway planning came from Secretary Hyde's decision; the nation was in the grips of a depression, and there were no funds for costly forest highways.

Residents of Fresno and Madera Counties were aware of the corridor and wouldn't forget its intended purpose. Politicians liked to imagine new purposes for their dream highway, among them serving the impending war. A *Fresno Bee* headline on February 19, 1939, read, "Maderans Back North Fork to Nevada Route." Citing fears of war in Europe that might bring American involvement, Fresno Chamber of Commerce President J. E. Barrett proposed a highway for transport of weapons to coastal bases from a storage depot in Hawthorne, Nevada.[14]

As the prospect of war loomed, President Franklin Roosevelt charged military leaders to reevaluate their existing resources and make haste with planning for mobilization. At the time, the nation's principal ammunition depots were located in New Jersey and in Nevada. Established in 1930, the Naval Ammunition Depot in Hawthorne, Nevada, was positioned far enough from the coast to avoid aerial attack, yet close enough to California ports. The depot was therefore linked by rail to major transportation routes, either north and west via Reno and Donner Summit or south and west via Las Vegas. Transfer of heavy ordnance required a year-round rail route, certainly not a mountain highway that was treacherous in winter.

Apparently unaware of these facts, the *Fresno Bee* followed up in August 1941 with news of impending legislation for construction of a road over Mammoth Pass, modernizing an existing road that had long serviced the lakes region above the town of Mammoth Lakes. Misunderstanding the geography, reporters were describing a different route by confusing Mammoth Pass on the southern shoulder of Mammoth Mountain with Minaret Summit at the north shoulder. Regardless of the confusion, nothing was ever heard from Washington military planners about the prospect of a new military route across the Sierra. The only strategic thoroughfare built in North America during World War II was the Alaskan Highway for supply and reinforcement of a region believed at the time to be at risk of Japanese invasion.[15]

Meanwhile, nobody knew how long the war would last, and when it did end, fear of continued economic depression limited any hope for a prompt financial recovery. Many could remember the deep recession that followed World War I. The foreseeable future left no prospect for growth; therefore, no wiggle room existed in Agriculture or Interior Department budgets. The notion of building another road across the Sierra was put aside—but not for long.

EARLY SIERRA CROSSINGS

*"We knew that California lay to the West,
and that was the extent of our knowledge."*
John Bidwell, 1841[16]

D ESPITE CALIFORNIA'S HISTORIC reputation for encouraging overland wagon routes, limiting barriers to railroad development, establishing a Bureau of Highways soon after the automobile was invented, and sponsoring drivable roads before most other states, its transportation agencies have always faced a daunting topography that includes the most forbidding geologic barrier in North America. The Sierra Nevada, a massive 360-mile long mountain wall extending from Mount Lassen southward to the Tehachapi Range, has stymied or stalled every mode of conveyance since Americans first inhabited their western landscape.

This formidable barrier emerged twice from recesses of the Earth's crust, first a range of comparable height (proto-Sierra) formed by a collision of tectonic plates and burial of molten magma as many as 100 million years ago. After a prolonged period of cooling and mountainous erosion, there was a second rising of gigantic blocks (plutons) of granitic rock (batholith) as recently as five million years ago that following volcanic activity, serial glaciers, and constant erosion provides the spectacular landscape we enjoy today.[17]

Anthropologists inform us that during the Pleistocene migration across the Bering Land Bridge, the most recent glaciers forced a divergence of native tribes, Washoe and Paiute to the east of a great mountain range; Maidu and Miwok to the west. When trade incentives became strong enough to prompt reciprocal transit, people inhabiting the eastern desert mingled peaceably and productively with natives living in the western foothills. Weather conditions permitting, the Miwoks traveled the mountains carrying acorns, berries, salmon, trout, baskets, and shells for use as beads to exchange with the Great Basin Paiute for pine nuts, insect larvae, salt, animal skins, and obsidian (volcanic glass) for use as arrowheads.[18]

From stories passed down over generations, we know where some of these native trade routes were located. Each summer descendants of the Mono Lake Paiutes begin a ritual forty-six–mile trek departing from their ancestral lake habitat, ascending the treacherous Bloody Canyon to cross at Mono Pass, then continuing along trails paralleling the modern Tioga Road before descending into Yosemite Valley where native trade fairs once convened. Another native route to the south served gold miners as the "Old French Trail."[19]

No evidence indicates that Spanish explorers ever crossed the mountain range to which they assigned its modern name. Juan Rodriguez Cabrillo is credited with sighting snow-capped mountains from his ship in Monterey Bay and naming them "Las Sierras Nevadas," (the snowy range). Owing to the Earth's curvature, he could not have seen the mountains we call the Sierra Nevada; Instead, he was looking at the Santa Cruz Mountains of the Pacific Coastal Range.[20]

Two centuries would pass before Spanish soldiers and their padres confronted the massive mountains that lay within Upper (Alta) California. Capt. Pedro Fages in 1772 described his ascent of Cajon Pass and traverse of the great desert beyond. From the vantage of Tejon Pass, he observed mountains perpetually covered with snow, probably the first recorded description of the Sierra

Nevada. Four years later, Franciscan missionaries Pedro Font and Francisco Garces placed the mountains on a map with additional descriptive detail. Military expeditions often ventured into the Central Valley in pursuit of natives stealing horses, but none reported challenging the mountain wall.

Jedediah Smith, a twenty-seven-year-old trapper from central New York, achieved lasting fame as the first white man to cross the Sierra Nevada. Departing Salt Lake in the summer of 1826, Smith's party headed south in front of the Wasatch Range, then turned west and entered Alta California through the vast Mojave Desert. Although welcomed at the San Gabriel Mission, Smith was not granted entry to lands beyond and north. Withdrawing to a place outside of Mexican jurisdiction, he and his party turned northward and advanced into the Central Valley. Attracting notice from troops based at the Presidio in San Francisco, his lame excuse—waiting for snow to melt—proved futile. Giving up plans to reach the Columbia River, he escaped to the east, crossing in the vicinity of Ebbetts Pass, then returning to Salt Lake.[21]

In 1833, Lt. Joseph Walker was one of three officers selected to lead parties of soldiers hired for trapping game. His orders limited him to territory immediately west of the Great Salt Lake, but he was determined to reach the Pacific Coast. Taking with him seventy men, including an intrepid clerk who recorded the venture, Walker followed the Humboldt River in northern Nevada, turned south toward the Carson River, and then went up into the mountains. His exact route is not clear, but two remarkable discoveries suggest the Walker party encountered the unique beauty of Yosemite, not by entering the valley, but rather viewing it from overlooks familiar to contemporary Tioga Road motorists.[22]

They witnessed "great streams of water plunging through chasms cut into mile high precipices." After working their way across ridges dividing the Tuolumne River from the Merced, they came upon "a grove filled with trees... incredibly large... measuring 16-18 fathoms about the trunk." This was perhaps the first recorded description of *Sequoia gigantea*.[23]

Walker and his party eventually reached the expansive valley that lay west of the mountains, then on to San Francisco where they hailed an American merchant ship willing to deposit them in Monterey. Unwilling to renavigate the High Sierra; they traveled south in search of a less difficult passage. They found it in the winding Kern River gorge that opens to a 5,250-foot pass now bearing Walker's name. Regrettably, Walker's retreat from the Eastern Sierra was marred by traumatic encounters with Paiute war parties. The resulting slaughter left natives with ample motive for aggressive resistance to future explorations.

First among the earliest pioneers seeking new lands to settle and cultivate was a group led by John Bidwell, who later admitted: "Our ignorance of the route was complete; we knew that California lay to the west and that was the extent of our knowledge." Among the earliest wagon trains to leave Missouri in 1841, their vehicles would not make it over the Sierra, a feat that awaited better understanding of the geography and better constructed wagons. According to one diarist, "we traveled for seven long and weary months with no guide and no compass, nothing but the sun to direct us. Wagons were jettisoned in Nevada, and our goods were converted to a pack train that reached the Sierra Nevada by October." Because the snow arrived late that year they crossed at Sonora Pass.[24]

The recorded journeys of Lt. John C. Fremont make for an interesting account of both territorial exploration and political opportunism. Notoriously overconfident, he enjoyed the patronage of a powerful father-in-law, Missouri senator Thomas Hart Benton. Collaborating with his wife, he produced an account of his 1842 Rocky Mountains explorations that became an international best seller. Departing again in May 1843 with orders to extend the prior year's survey, he arrived at the Truckee River, turned southwest, and climbed out of Carson Valley. While pausing near present-day Markleeville, he took an advance party up a distant peak, looked northward, and saw a "grand lake tucked between two ridges." It was the first recorded sighting of what we know today as Lake Tahoe.

For his return journey, Fremont avoided the Sierra crest, preferring to take his party south and over Walker Pass, which he missed entirely, crossing at the Tehachapi Pass instead. An erroneous description of his course of travel would contribute to

Sierra Nevada's Ritter Range, "...the most divine of mountain ranges." according to John Muir
CREDIT: *Stephen Ingram*

confusion among travelers for years to come. Continuing into Nevada, he wrote in his diary that most of the land between Salt Lake
and the Sierra Nevada was "like a great basin containing lakes and
rivers that find no outlet to the sea," a geographic designation still
in popular use.

The plight of the Donner party, which left thirty-five of
eighty-four emigrants dead, is mentioned only in passing, not because the course they took was unique but instead to highlight the
scale of disaster that results from poor judgment and bad timing.
Choosing to accept questionable advice about a trail that delayed
their mountain arrival and then having to deal with early winter

conditions meant there was no way out of heartbreak. Successful Sierra crossings were based then as now on geography, a respect for climatic variations, and proper timing.[25]

As Fremont departed California and crossed the parched basin he so aptly named, numerous wagon ruts were already visible. The age of exploration was giving way to a new era of western migration, with heavy reliance on wheeled vehicles. Emigrants bound for California followed the Platte and Sweetwater Rivers, crossed the Rockies at South Pass in Wyoming, drove westward north of the Salt Lake, and reached the Humboldt River's diminishing stream that ended in Humboldt Sink. This was one of the many low elevations in the Great Basin where thirst might cost lives. At this point two choices were available: 1) Find and follow the Truckee River to a broad meadow—the future site of Reno, Nevada—ascend the Truckee Gorge to Lake Tahoe, then climb the sheer face of a rocky pass that would forever bear the name of the Donner party; or 2) Follow an easier emigrant route southward, find and ascend the Carson River Valley, then cross south of Lake Tahoe via Carson Pass, a path chosen by General Fremont.[26]

In 1849, California suddenly became a magnet for anybody willing to pull up stakes, endure several months onboard ship or suffer weeks of hardship crossing overland by wagon, all for the mystical prospect of sudden wealth in the gold fields. Few succeeded but many remained to pursue alternate trades. One hundred thousand–plus arrived between 1848 and 1850, and an equal number over the next two years, half by land and half by sea. Because prospectors generally believed they would strike it rich and never go back, there was little motive for building or maintaining roads. That stimulus would come later from merchants in need of reliable supply channels. Stagecoach companies flourished briefly, bringing news from home or transporting wives, until the railroads came. Highway opportunists of all stripes functioned at the same time, either as individuals or in monopolistic partnership, bent on upgrading a road or repairing a bridge in return for tolls.[27]

Toll roads of the 1850s were gradually replaced by "public roads," which meant paying by subscription for repeated use of a particular road, all proceeds applied to maintaining surfaces and replacing washed-out bridges. When California became the thirty-first state, its legislature encountered immediate pressure for a road-building program based on tax revenues. Early proposals led to endless bickering over which of the many competing trans-Sierra routes would receive funding. California's first "Act to Construct a Wagon Road Over the Sierra Nevada," passed on April 28, 1855, did not even specify a preferred route. Furthermore, the functionally useless law discouraged new roads by restricting appropriations to existing wagon roads. Political paralysis in Sacramento actually hastened the building of a railroad across the Sierra Nevada.

The model American demonstration of entrepreneurial zeal was the Central Pacific Railroad, along with its four calculating partners. Talk of a railroad across the continent began in the 1830s with the building of regional lines in the northeast. Decisive action awaited resolution of the north-south conflict. Neither faction wanted the other to gain advantage in terms of electoral representation, economic stimulus, or population growth. California's congressional delegation was instructed to urge passage of any kind of national railroad act, assuming that wherever the chosen route lay geographically, the enterprise would terminate somewhere in California.

By the time a workable course for the first transcontinental railroad was selected, the Carson route had long dominated the Truckee route. But railroad engineer Theodore Judah recognized inherent topographic advantages to a rail line over Donner Summit. Judah's entrée for making that decision for Californians was his success building the Sacramento Valley Railroad. And at the age of twenty-eight, he had also engineered the Niagara Gorge Railroad without mishap.

Captivated by the challenge of finding railroad friendly terrain, Judah tirelessly hiked the Sierra foothills with his wife. She sketched while he studied the topography. But it was a druggist in Dutch Flat who found what Judah was searching for: a continuous ridge that ascended at constant rate to his community at 3,200 feet without any grade redundancy (ups and downs). Furthermore, the same ridge continued its steady climb until reaching Donner

Summit. That single geographic discovery helped Judah convince important people in 1860 that a railroad could be built. This led to incorporation of the Central Pacific Railroad by four unlikely partners—Collis Huntington, Mark Hopkins, Charles Crocker, and Leland Stanford—all of them Sacramento storekeepers with a common dream but no prior railroading experience. The "Big Four," as they were called, were entirely dependent on Judah for achieving their goal. Nearly a decade would pass before the golden spike was driven at Promontory, Utah, uniting the westbound Union Pacific and the eastbound Central Pacific.[28]

Only one Sierra rail crossing prevailed until 1909 when the Western Pacific Railroad completed a second line over Beckwourth Pass and through the canyon of the Feather River. The original Donner trail bed was eventually abandoned for a new route that exploits a tunnel excavated through aptly named Mount Judah. The original grades and snow sheds remain visible over US 40 as historic landmarks and a tribute to the labor of Chinese emigrants. Today, these two mountain rail routes dominate east-west shipping north of Los Angeles and south of the Pacific Northwest. The Sierra Nevada still protects its barrier role.

For vehicular traffic, there are many more choices, all with rich historic traditions. The summit named for the Donner party served mostly as a wagon road for logistical support of railroad construction. Later called the Dutch Flat and Donner Wagon Road, it fared poorly because it couldn't serve the traveler or the shipper as well as the railroad could. In time it became a segment of US 40, and in the 1960s it received a brand new Interstate 80, serving today as one of the busiest thoroughfares in the nation. The Lake Tahoe Wagon Route served as a toll road until 1886 when Eldorado County transformed it into a public highway. Since the launch of California's Bureau of Highways in 1896, the Lake Tahoe Wagon Route became the first state highway. After major bridge repairs in 1917 it became State Highway 11, and following inauguration of the federal system for numbering highways, US 50.

The Carson Pass route endured countless realignments. The original emigrant trail has been moved both north and south according to the whims of road builders, who have used in their design Carson Pass, West Pass, Squaw Ridge, or Iron Mountain Ridge. Today, only twenty miles of the original traverse remain a part of modern State Highway 88. The Sonora route, previously called the Sierra-Mono Wagon Road, served only a few emigrants until 1859 when it became a major supply route for gold rush communities east of the Sierra, especially Bodie and Aurora. Following decades of service as a toll road and then a subscription highway, it became State Highway 108, open for all but the winter months when heavy snow forces closure.

When the notion of putting another road over the Sierra near Mammoth Lakes was first heard, there were ten highways crossing the range. This fact alone reinforced the positions of two fiercely opposed factions. One asked, "Because there are ten, why not have one more?" The other said, "Because there are already ten, why build another?"

A DESTINATION RESORT

MODERN-DAY MAMMOTH LAKES, California, continues to consider itself a prime Eastern Sierra destination resort. Its elected officials devote all the tax revenues they can justify, sometimes more, to expanding services at the regional airport. The idea is hardly a new one; business leaders began thinking of their community as a destination resort when postwar Mammoth Lakes was becoming a haven for alpine skiers. But in the 1960s, instead of worrying about the airport, local citizens were voicing opposition to the prospect of another trans-Sierra highway, one that might penetrate the very heart of their community.

According to his friends, local developer Tom Dempsey was first to apply the term "destination resort" to Mammoth Lakes: "a place people should travel to and not just through." Sporting goods retailer Doug Kittredge put in writing his own opposition to the road: "Having a main highway through the center of town will eliminate Mammoth as a destination resort and relegate it to a mere spot on the road." Recalling his years as president of the Mammoth Lakes Chamber of Commerce (1965–69), Ervin "Chip" Van Nattan recalled very few supporters of the idea. Owners of Mammoth Mountain Inn, for example, stood to gain from increased traffic; their property sat across from the main lifts in the path of the proposed highway. And so they demonstrated their support at hearings in Sacramento. Meanwhile, the Mammoth Lakes Chamber of Commerce never wavered from its resistance despite intense political pressure.[29]

In slightly less than a century Mammoth had repeatedly transformed itself from a short-lived mining district (1875–80) to a lasting pastoral meadow community (1900–37) and ultimately to a determined forerunner of the modern resort community it represents today. Throughout these transitions, geography, climate, and heritage have played major defining roles.[30]

Prospectors who returned in 1877 for a second look at the Mammoth Lakes Basin brought with them Gen. George S. Dodge, who according to a *San Francisco Daily Exchange* reporter "had an inkling there was a solid mountain of gold quartz somewhere up back of the Yosemite." Whether Dodge's reputation as a mining investor was based on proven success or merely a knack for capital formation is not clear. In any event, when Dodge was shown a particular ridge called "Mineral Hill," without a moment's hesitation he declared it "the largest bonanza outside of Virginia City." With preliminary assay reports in hand and presumed to be accurate, he announced that a "deal could be made" which in that day meant selling speculative shares to as many unwary investors as could be found. The resulting enterprise, incorporated in 1878, was appropriately named the Mammoth Mining Company.[31]

A nearby volcanic peak, known then as Pumice Mountain, was perceived by prospectors to be mammoth just like the mining company; so it became Mount Mammoth and later Mammoth Mountain. The first inhabitation of Mineral Hill therefore became Mammoth City, whose population exploded to twenty-five hundred inside of a year. From four prospective tunnels came sacks of prime quartz, all forwarded with dispatch to nearby Benton for assay. When a favorable report was returned, Mammoth Mining Company shares leaped from three dollars to ten dollars a share overnight. Dodge had already purchased five claims for ten thousand dollars cash plus thirty thousand dollars in company stock at the opening price. Records fail to reveal how much equity he took for himself before the venture folded.

More than a century later, there is no convincing evidence that gold in any significant quantity was extracted from Mineral Hill at that time. Because of high iron content, the ridge is known today as Red Mountain. But throughout its thousand days of glory, Mineral Hill loomed over three distinct communities: Mammoth City, where most of the ore was extracted; Pine City, facing nearby Lake Mary from which water needed for operations was drawn; and Mill City, where a twenty-stamp mill was built for processing ore. More than three thousand miners came to work the claims, build flumes for water diversion, operate a tramway for transporting ore, maintain the giant mill, and manage all the hotels, saloons, and brothels needed for support of the encampment.[32]

But it was snow, dozens of feet of snow, plus rapidly diminishing mining yields, that proved the undoing of Dodge's speculative bonanza. Most of the district's intrepid settlers vacated the area within three years, all but a few cowhands who drove cattle from Owens Valley into the upper mountain meadows and then back. They pitched tents just down hill from Mill City and called it Mineral Park. Later they built cabins in the picturesque meadows below, a settlement they called Mammoth Camp.[33]

Long after the futile rush for gold had run its course, a different kind of pioneer entered the Eastern Sierra with plans to establish a year-round community, according to Old Mammoth historian Adele Reed. "They came riding their funny old cars . . . Fords and Chevies [sic] and other makes," she wrote. The new century brought new modes of transportation, on roads more suited for horse and wagon than for vehicles powered by engines. Upon arrival in Mammoth Camp, they either continued to sleep in their vehicles or they pitched tents. Only a few could afford to stay at the newly opened Wildasinn Hotel. Fully taken by the grandeur of the mountains, seasonal visitors found excuses to return and settle permanently, identify useful work, and build cabins that could withstand the winter season. More hotels were established together with taverns and markets and the community's first "auto repair garage."[34]

At no time were Mammoth Camp's residents separated from a transportation network. Wagon roads had existed in the valleys east of the Sierra Nevada since the 1850s. Pine City had served as eastern terminus pack route from Fresno flats. Little more than a trail, it served the mule trains that hauled supplies from California's Central Valley. Both prospectors and freight from San Francisco entered the Eastern Sierra over the Carson and Sonora Passes wagon roads via Bodie. Heavy equipment for the mines and an occasional crate of fresh-picked fruit came up the Owens River Valley from Los Angeles via the city of Mojave. Entering the high country north of Bishop required use of a toll road. First constructed by J. L. C. Sherwin and partners in the 1870s, the road underwent countless upgrades and rerouting but retains to this day its original identity as Sherwin Grade. Always vulnerable to rock falls and drifting snow, it rises from 4,000 to 7,000 feet in just over nine miles.

With the arrival of touring automobiles and their stalwart operators came private associations for the promotion of safer roads. The Inyo Good Road Club first convened in the spring of 1910, and by August it had persuaded governor James Gillett to visit the Eastern Sierra, dedicate a one-mile segment of model road construction south of Big Pine, and promise state support for better road surfaces between Mojave and Bridgeport. First christened "El Camino Sierra," it later became State Highway 23 and in 1935, US 395.[35]

Two wagon roads that paralleled Sherwin and Mammoth Creeks provided access to Mammoth Camp from the main highway. In Mammoth they joined as Old Mammoth Road, the community's main thoroughfare. The Lakes Basin above Mammoth Camp could be reached by the same steep switchback that originally serviced the mining district. In 1920, work began on Lake Mary Road, a more gradual ascent cut into a southeast-facing slope of Mammoth Mountain. This project was budgeted by the US Forest Service (USFS) at four thousand dollars but also attracted contributions from local residents because the new road allowed for easy access to several picturesque lakes, prompting development of several summer resorts. Tamarack Lodge on Twin Lakes, Crystal Crag Lodge on Lake Mary, Wildyrie Lodge on Lake Mamie, and Wood's Lodge on Lake George remain popular to this day.[36]

In 1933, Mammoth Lakes residents learned from Division of Highways officials that plans for a new road might reposition their community again. An entirely new access road coming off El Camino Real would bypass the meadow. Completed in 1937, State Highway 112 (later CA 203) took origin from US 395 at Casa Diablo Hot Springs, a popular native gathering place for centuries and today a modern geothermal power-generating facility. The new highway, today's Main Street, penetrated largely undeveloped land before connecting with Lake Mary Road. Old Mammoth Road was later redirected to join the new thoroughfare. Recognizing that the intersection would become the epicenter of a relocated community, Frank and Norah Penney moved their bakery to the southwest corner of Old Mammoth Road and Main Street, named it first Penney's Tavern and later Mammoth Tavern. With rooms to let and housekeeping cabins, plus a well-stocked bar and restaurant, it became the place to be in a revitalized Village of Mammoth Lakes. Before a post office was built, all mail came to the Mammoth Tavern lobby where it was spread on a table for locals to rummage through, hoping something was addressed to them.[37]

ALTHOUGH SKIS HAD been used by power company surveyors in the gold fields of California to facilitate year-round mining, Alpine skiing as we know it today did not become a recreational sport until the early twentieth century. Shortly after the Yosemite Valley's Awahnee Hotel opened in 1927, a ski school was established to help attract guests during the winter season. Travel guides for Inyo and Mono Counties illustrated happy skiers in front of a Mammoth Camp hotel. H. F. Rey and family, transplanted from Switzerland to California, began visiting Mammoth Camp in 1926, returning each winter to hike up Mammoth Mountain and descend on skis. They rarely saw any other skiers until the mid-1930s.[38]

Essential for determining the destiny of Alpine skiing in the Eastern Sierra was the 1928 arrival of Edna McCoy and her thirteen-year-old son, Dave, for a visit with friends living near Independence, California. Abandoned by the boy's father, she was grateful for an opportunity to introduce her son to the congeniality and stability of a high desert family and to the beauty of the surrounding mountains. Enthralled by the geography, Dave McCoy later had this to say: "I couldn't get over the snow on the mountains in the middle of July. A spiritual feeling came over me, also a sense of opportunity and desire. I felt like I belonged and I knew I would come back." Come back he did, several times during subsequent summer breaks from school.

On one of those trips, he met a team of hydrographers working for the Los Angeles Department of Water and Power (DWP). Dave already knew how to ski, one of the qualifications for a field job. What could be more fun, he asked himself, than measuring the Sierra Nevada snowpack and calculating seasonal variations. It was not a surprise then to find a graduating Dave McCoy forsake four football scholarships, hitch rides back to Independence, and begin his working career at Jim's Place, a popular restaurant in the heart of town. Dave washed dishes and bused tables while his mother cooked. Advancing to soda jerk, he spotted a pretty blonde one afternoon, a standout among several cheerleaders from Bishop High School. Two years later, chance favored him another meeting; her name was Roma Carriere. They dated four years before marrying in 1941 and settling temporarily in Bishop. While working as a DWP laborer, Dave passed exams required to qualify as a hydrographer. His first assignment came with a bungalow perched on a hill overlooking Crowley Lake near Mammoth Lakes. Roma was soon pregnant.[39]

What mattered most to McCoy, next to his family, was skiing. He likened the Sierra Nevada to the Tyrolean Alps, even though he had never been to Europe. "Along 395 for a hundred miles, you can ski anywhere," he was heard to say. Together with friends, he installed the first rope tow in the Eastern Sierra near Independence. The year was 1936. "We jacked up a truck, slipped a rope over the rear tire rim and tightened it against an uphill pulley." Later at McGee Mountain north of Crowley, "we used a differential from a discarded vehicle, cut one axle out, capped it, turned it vertically, and attached the drive shaft to the bed of a Model A truck, then hung a winch attached to a wheel farther uphill."

McCoy already knew the most about weather conditions in the vicinity of Mammoth Mountain, and along with his grasp of machinery, he became the alchemist who could turn snow into gold. He had first skied Mammoth Mountain with the Rey family in 1938. Climbing to the 11,000-foot summit, he looked westward and saw the low points in the Sierra Crest through which moisture-laden cold fronts could dump great quantities of snow on the mountain slopes below him. The barren summit cornice held a lip of ice and snow that loomed over its vertical chutes. McCoy committed to memory every contour of the mountain and realized there was more than any network of temporary rope lifts could service. He knew the first powered chair lift was just installed at Sun Valley, Idaho. "Why not at Mammoth?" McCoy asked himself. In 1938, he already knew what the destiny of Mammoth Mountain's terrain would be.

Just as motoring frenzy had spawned associations promoting drivable roads, skiers formed their own clubs that supported the use of uphill lifts. So there was an Independence Ski Club, an Eastern Sierra Ski Club based in Bishop, a Mono Ski Club at June Mountain, and in time a Mammoth Mountain Ski Club. Meanwhile, the slopes off McGee Mountain became the Eastern Sierra's center for ski racing. A natural teacher and state competition winner himself, McCoy nurtured the development of young racers, some of whom would later compete nationally and internationally.

Success and accolades notwithstanding, McCoy's focus was on Mammoth Mountain, but there were two problems: access and competition. Hans George, an Austrian ski instructor, maintained a lift and warming hut on a southeast-facing slope just off Lake Mary Road. McCoy preferred the north-facing slope that required a six-mile trek up Minaret Road from the village. During years of heavy snow, the north face was unapproachable. But on a pleasant sunny Sunday early in December 1941, Dave and Roma McCoy were there operating their lift when a nearby radio interrupted its music for an announcement. The news from Hawaii stunned them both and everyone nearby. Pearl Harbor Sunday foretold a new way of life for young and old alike. The McCoys called it a day, shut down the lift, bid farewell to friends, and did not return to Mammoth Mountain for nearly five years.

Practically no one was expecting the economic boom that came after a victorious army of eight million returned home to resume their lives and begin spending their military earnings.

Factories throughout the nation converted their assembly lines from weapons to refrigerators and washing machines. Government agencies such as the USFS anticipated a surge in forest recreation, including Alpine skiing. An aerial survey of potential ski areas in California, Nevada, and Idaho inexplicably omitted Mammoth Mountain from its ranking sites. Experts believed there to be too much elevation, too much wind and snow, and too great an avalanche risk. If that wasn't enough, the mountain was poorly shaped, making it difficult to funnel skiers into a base area. And one more problem: Mammoth Mountain was too far away from population centers.[40]

At least two people disagreed with the mountain's low ranking: District Ranger Fred Meckel and rope tow operator Dave McCoy. Experience had shown that people from Southern California didn't mind the drive up US 395. McCoy was convinced the slopes were entirely suitable for enjoyable skiing, and he was confident that winter resort development throughout the nation would yield effective technology for avalanche control. Ranger Meckel soon went to bat for the required USFS approval.

WITHIN A YEAR following the war's end, the campaign for another trans-Sierra highway resumed. "Road Still Needed," declared the *Fresno Bee* in its June 18, 1946, edition. Citing an initiative by the Madera and Fresno Counties Chambers of Commerce, editorial writers urged immediate funding for the first twenty-five-mile segment of a proposed "Mammoth Pass Road." Favoring commercial advantage instead of strategic military need, they focused on the potential for harvesting two million board feet of timber plus an equivalent yield of pulp for the paper industry. Tungsten and iron ore were reported to exist in large quantities.[41]

Once again, the western slope parvenus of highway planning were showing their misunderstanding of eastern geography and geology. Mammoth Pass lay south of Mammoth Mountain and Minaret Summit was to the north. Mammoth Pass hadn't been serviced by any road since the French Trail functioned as a pack route. Minaret Summit, a mountain pass and not a peak, was presently serviced by an unimproved forest road. As for the imagined abundance of metallic ore, nothing significant was proved then or discovered since.

Meanwhile, by 1947 Dave McCoy reestablished towing operations on Mammoth Mountain. To meet the "too much snow" problem, he purchased six war-surplus Army Weasels, a track vehicle designed for Allied operations in Europe. Ideal for transporting skiers over deep snow, they were difficult to maintain. Countless hours of midweek maintenance were needed to make them functional on weekends. Reliable access meant larger crowds and increased lift revenue. McCoy later recalled days when snowfall impeded visibility and skiers hanging on to a towrope followed the Weasels down winding Minaret Road into town. Whether this application of military technology could persuade authorities to change their minds about a ski resort on Mammoth Mountain remained to be seen.[42]

Less concerned about growing interest in a ski resort, Sierra Club Executive Director David Brower and board member Ike Livermore fought and won their battle to change the organization's position on wilderness roads. A new policy statement issued in 1947 left no doubt: "There is no justification for dividing a priceless wilderness; therefore, no new road building across the Sierra!" Livermore had been unaware of any alleged military purpose for building another Sierra crossing, but he understood why agencies like the National Park Service, whose goal was to facilitate public access to natural wonders, and the USFS, long committed to its multiple use doctrine, might continue to push for road improvements.

In 1956, David Brower spoke to a joint meeting of the Fresno and Madera County Boards of Supervisors. He urged spokesmen of these organizations to accurately reflect the Sierra Club's current position on road building: "The public interest is best served if no trans-Sierra roads are built between Tioga and Walker passes, that the wilderness zone between remain unspoiled so that future generations might be granted the right to decide whether they can afford to preserve this unique expanse." In that room, his message fell on deaf ears. And his unwelcome message came at a time when the US Congress was deliberating the Interstate Defense Highway

Act, a potentially massive source of highway funding that politicians could not ignore.[43]

No surprise then that the nation's defense needs surfaced once again as justification for the desired highway. The Cold War was now on everybody's mind, and Fresno and Madera citizens believed they were entitled to an escape route. According to Madera Supervisor Carl W. McCollister, the road was, "necessary to give people in the San Joaquin Valley their rightful highway outlet to the east should coastal cities become targets of nuclear attack." One local mused that if Valley folks wanted it, it wouldn't happen in twenty-five years; if Los Angeles wanted it, then it could happen in two years.[44]

As soon as the 1956 Interstate Highway bill passed, the United States Bureau of Public Roads announced that a preliminary survey of a proposed trans-Sierra highway by way of Mammoth Pass would be conducted over succeeding months. By December, the USFS learned that actual field studies awaited the seasonal snowmelt but that aerial photos and geological surveys were already under way. According to the *Fresno Bee*, "California might be in store for a large share of the multi-millions allocated for highway development."[45]

A time had come for opponents of the road to be heard. One welcome voice of dissent was the renowned Sierra Nevada photographer Ansel Adams. In collaboration with Fresno insurance executive Floyd Lobree, he agreed to co-chair a newly formed Sierra Resources Committee dedicated to opposing any further road development in the Sierra Nevada. The time had also come for citizens of Mammoth Lakes to gather their forces in opposition to what might represent another sweeping transformation of their community, one that few wished to experience.[46]

IV

"DEAR PEOPLE, START WRITING LETTERS"

G ENNY SMITH CAN remember when her twenty-seven-year campaign against the Minaret Summit Road began, not just the day—December 5, 1958—but the exact moment when she took pen in hand and wrote to as many people eager to fight the road issue as she could think of: "Dear people, Start writing letters!"[47]

The *Bakersfield Californian* had just reported the feasibility, according to highway authorities, of a new road across the Sierra. She wanted her letter to reflect how this kind of validation might energize the resolve of road advocates. The news article was based on a long-awaited report commissioned in 1956 by three cooperating agencies, the Bureau of Public Roads, the US Forest Service, and the California Division of Highways. Western States Regional Engineer Sheridan Farin qualified his report's tentative conclusion by noting that a detailed location survey would follow. Genny Smith wondered what he meant by "feasible" and how could a mountain highway be declared feasible without completing a location survey first? "But what did I know about highways?" she asked. In time she learned a great deal about them. And she would establish her reputation for tenacity and factual precision by posing questions no one else thought to ask.[48]

In a more jubilant tone, the *Fresno Bee* reported that the Mammoth Pass Road was now backed by a federal agency with important consequences for the state and for local communities. Quoting Farin, chamber of commerce president Lee Balotti, apparently unconcerned about the absence of location studies, revealed that the road would be a class B forest highway.[49]

In her plea for the writing of letters, Smith explained she didn't have in mind a torrent of unfocused pleadings falling on legislator's desks. It wasn't time for that yet. Instead, she wanted everybody to write to the same person, Chief Engineer Farin, and ask for a copy of the full report. "If you're told copies are not available, ask them to give reasons why they shouldn't be made available," she added. "Remind them you are a taxpayer, a Mammoth property owner, etc." Smith had anticipated correctly that the Bureau of Public Roads was unprepared to share any of their reports with the general public. Farin would later acknowledge that demand for this particular report exceeded both the capacity of his mimeograph machine and his annual postage budget.[50]

Bureaucratic encounters of this variety inspired a number of Mammoth Lakes citizens to form their own advocacy group. They suspected that big-picture organizations such as the Sierra Club were unlikely to achieve the outcome they wanted. The name they chose, Mono County Resources Committee, was intentionally vague. Their only administrative formality was a post office box and a letterhead with an understated motto, "Thoughtful Progress." These modest initiatives belied the persuasive power they would eventually wield. Meeting infrequently and only in the homes of members, they generated thousands of letters. At the very heart of this coordinated effort stood Genny Smith.

Born Genevieve Hall in San Francisco, raised in Portland, and educated at Reed College, she graduated with a degree in political science. While looking for "just the right job," war intervened. Opting for service with the Red Cross, she was assigned to one of Utah's largest hospitals at Kearns Army Air Base near Salt Lake City. Just forty-five minutes from Alta, she "learned to ski really well." Moving to Bakersfield, California, after the war she taught school and married a geologist. Bakersfield had a ski club, so it wasn't long before she and her husband discovered Mammoth Mountain and fell for the area. "It was winters and summers thereafter," she later recalled. Quick to say she wasn't a permanent resident of Mammoth Lakes, she might as well have been; most of her Mammoth friends had always thought of her as a "local." [51]

Returning over the span of several decades, she explored most corners of the Eastern Sierra on foot, systematically recording her observations. Along with carefully selected experts, she compiled and published *Mammoth Lakes Sierra* in 1959. Now in its seventh edition, it has long served as the most popular guide to the region. The success of her first book led to publication of others dealing with the history and natural beauty of the Eastern Sierra. So Smith was not susceptible to obfuscation based on false claims of road expertise, especially when they were unsupported by facts or geographic reality. She greeted every road-promoting document as a challenge to common sense and then proceeded to conduct her own research as thoroughly as she had done for her books. Always prepared with questions, she knew how to ask them repeatedly if necessary until she elicited an answer or an admission of folly. What precisely are the needs, if any, for such a road? What are the genuine costs of construction? What about continuing maintenance? Fair weather or all-season route, and if the latter, what will be the annual cost of snow removal, a factor left out of most early proposals. What sources of funding for the putative highway? Which budget would be responsible for maintenance? After she uncovered answers lacking in validity, she would distribute her findings far and wide.

"Genny was our scribe, always taking notes and writing letters," mused Bob Schotz, a local businessman who believes to this day that victory would have eluded the community without her determination. "No matter what season we were in or where she was located, her heart remained with the road issue. She grabbed on and never let go of it."

"Nonsense," counters Smith, remembering the road battle. "I was only a 'tree-hugger' in the eyes of politicians and they usually pay no mind to us. It was businessmen like Bob who made the difference," she added. "This road was a business proposition from

Genny Smith and friend holding 1st edition of *Mammoth Lakes Sierra*
CREDIT: *Genny Smith*

Bob and Peggy Schotz, Proprietors, Woods Lodge on Lake George
CREDIT: *Bob Schotz*

Lou and Marye Roeser at Mammoth Pack Station
CREDIT: *Marye Roeser*

the get-go and a poor one at that. He and his colleagues knew it
and were willing to stand up and say so."[52]

Schotz was one of several businessmen—including Doug
Kittredge and Tom Dempsey—who loved the area and understood
what would be good for the town and the natural environment
alike. Schotz's parents were cause for his first visit to Mammoth in
1940, but he was responsible for returning the next year and finding a job at Tamarack Lodge on Twin Lakes. At sixteen he was giv-
en an unlikely assignment: run the laundry operation, a task he
performed well enough to be asked to return the following season. Following naval service in the Pacific, he earned a degree from
UC–Santa Barbara but continued to work summers in Mammoth
Lakes. Teaching vocational skills in Los Angeles for one year convinced him he belonged in the Eastern Sierra. Returning in 1951,

he and a partner bought Wood's Lodge on Lake George, a resort still operated by the Schotz family. As a developer and builder of homes, Schotz left his mark on the Mammoth Lakes community and recalls nearly everybody he has met during his career. But he likes the road story best because the outcome was so gratifying.

Equally committed to the road campaign were Lou and Marye Roeser along with Marye's sister Dorothy and brother-in-law Louis Fitzhugh. Lou Roeser, comfortable with horses since he was a child, came to Mammoth Lakes from Arizona in 1952 and worked as mule packer at Mammoth Lakes Pack Outfit near Lake Mary. Marye Russell worked at Camp High Sierra, a family camp owned and operated by the Los Angeles Department of Parks. Marye guided camp guests on horseback rides out of the pack station where Lou worked. They married and eventually purchased the pack outfit where they first met. Their love of the Sierra made for an easy decision to live there permanently. Dorothy, who taught history, circulated the first of many citizen petitions voicing opposition to the road.[53]

LITTLE OF SUBSTANCE came of the 1958 highway feasibility study, other than prompting from Central Valley factions random public gestures in support of the road. Regional engineer Farin never responded fully to the questions Genny Smith and her accomplices put to him. Defining an authentic need for the road was never easy. Fresno attorney and chamber of commerce spokesman Chester Warlow tried to exploit a comment made by National Park Service director Conrad Wirth, which was that another road across the Sierra might take pressure off the Tioga Pass Road. While it was true that the Tioga Road could not at the time withstand heavy trucking, plans were established to spend millions improving the road, particularly the segment east of Tioga Pass. When completed, however, the road would still require winter closure. Any new highway capable of displacing traffic from Tioga Pass would need to be open year-round, and workable specifications for such a venture did not exist.[54]

In fall of 1959, associate Supreme Court justice William O. Douglas arrived in the Sierra Nevada for a six-day trek organized for him by Sierra Club executive David Brower. With the justice on foot and his wife on horseback, a party that included Genny Smith departed from June Lake bound for Garnet Lake, which lay in the eastern shadow of Mount Ritter and Mount Banner, a segment of the Sierra Nevada that John Muir considered the most divine of mountain ranges. Asked for comment on the road issue, Douglas said, "Another road would be the worst thing that could happen here; all road building into wilderness areas must cease." The event had attracted the national press, who produced the wanted headlines, for example, "Justice Douglas Opposes Highway." [55]

Unable to accompany the justice on his backcountry adventure, Brower later spoke to the Fresno Chamber of Commerce, all of whose members were road promoters. "We do have a choice regarding the Mammoth road," he told them. "We no longer have a choice regarding the Donner, Echo, Carson, Ebbetts, Monitor, Sonora, Tioga, and Walker Passes. Long ago people made these choices for us. We take our position on behalf of those not yet born who will surely appreciate preservation of California's wilderness." Brower was building on a theme previously offered to a similar audience but achieved little. Soon afterward, the Fresno Chamber of Commerce rededicated its backing for an "All Year Sierra Road," through what was now being called "The Mammoth Corridor." [56]

Believing that what was needed to resolve the highway issue was a bigger Yosemite Park that incorporated the corridor, Sterling Cramer was a new voice on the matter. Cramer, speaking for the private operator of Yosemite concessions, proposed that primitive areas adjacent to the park be annexed so that the Ritter Range could be "maintained at the high standards of national parks." Hardly impartial on the issue, his idea was greeted favorably by the *Fresno Bee* editorial page even though prospects for one agency giving up territorial jurisdiction to another were remote. Nothing was heard again from USFS or NPS about annexation. [57]

By early 1960, it was clear the issue could not be resolved through locally organized efforts; the matter would require legislative action and this meant hearings, lots of them. The process began in 1961 with passage of State Senate Joint Resolution 43 to include the Mammoth Pass Road in the Forest Highway system, and for this the Bureau of Public Roads was obligated to conduct hearings in Fresno, Madera, Inyo, and Mono Counties. Objections to hearings on the issue were filed by the Sierra Club, the Wilderness Society, and the Nature Conservancy but to no avail. The first was held on May 16, 1961, in the Fresno County School Administration Building, and it was attended by Genny Smith, who took copious notes. Testimony included a history of the gap between primitive forest areas for the eventual purpose of building a road. The union of two forest highways (FH 74 and FH 81) was debated; the outcome was designation of a single forest highway: FH 100. Voices of advocacy included a mother who spoke of citizens having an "inalienable right to have fresh lettuce brought by truckers," a confounding plea because lettuce was most likely to come from the adjacent Central Valley than from the Eastern Sierra.[58]

Opinions about the road weren't unanimous even in Mammoth Lakes. The town's leading citizen, Dave McCoy, hadn't taken sides on the highway issue and never would. His fence-sitting posture derived from the success of his dream for Mammoth Mountain and an unwillingness to fight any measure that would diminish access to the expanding ski area. In 1953, McCoy had finally received his first twenty-five-year lease to operate a winter recreational area on Mammoth Mountain. Despite his financial weakness the fact that he was the only applicant for a permit might have helped, but victory was also based on the high opinion local foresters held for McCoy, his team, and his prospects. The government's decision proved wise; by 1965, the California Division of Highways would record three hundred and fifty thousand winter season visitors to Mammoth Mountain Ski Area (MMSA).

Shortly after the lease was signed, the state paved Minaret Road up to Minaret Summit, including a parking lot adjacent to the first warming hut constructed by McCoy's band of volunteers. Soon after, Dave and twelve carefully selected helpers essentially taught themselves how to install a chair lift, an extraordinary feat using components acquired with a handshake and a promise. With the resulting tow fees in hand, McCoy paid for that equipment ahead of schedule. The chosen dozen became the operations staff, and MMSA became the only ski area in the nation capable of installing its own lifts, more than two dozen by the end of the century.

The Town of Mammoth Lakes was gradually becoming a community dedicated entirely to recreational pursuits. Hotels and restaurants flourished. Mammoth Tavern at the intersection of Main Street and Old Mammoth Road was replaced by a shopping center that included a chain grocer, pharmacy, hardware store, laundromat, and a major bank. All of this was happening in concert with steady residential property growth. Year-round population in Mammoth Lakes grew along with the ski enterprise. Even if Dave McCoy wasn't going to speak out against a trans-Sierra road, he was the catalyst for the community's evolving self-esteem and willingness to determine its own fate.

Mammoth Lake's self-reliance notwithstanding, there was still plenty of momentum behind the road proposal, with a formidable new advocate in Bernice "Bernie" F. Sisk. Elected in 1955 as US representative for the Sixteenth District, including the cities of Fresno, Merced, and Modesto, he was a Democrat who managed to upset his district's longstanding Republican tradition. He quickly distinguished himself as a vigorous advocate for the Central Valley and would serve twelve consecutive terms. Instrumental in creating the Central Valley Project that still supplies water to the San Joaquin Valley, it was only a matter of time before his attention was drawn to the trans-Sierra road issue.[59]

Congressman Sisk's enthusiastic support was first reported by the *Fresno Bee* on November 18, 1964, as a call for accelerated funding of the necessary preliminary studies. Statements from Sisk and his staff reflected careful study of the appropriate maps and a clear understanding of the pertinent geography. For example, Sisk was careful to speak only of a "Minaret Summit Road" and not a "Mammoth Pass Road." He understood the practical difference between a native trade route and an existing forest highway. It made political sense to improve a functioning thoroughfare, especially one that was under federal jurisdiction. Reporters got the message too; newspaper references to a "Mammoth Pass Road" seemed to vanish overnight.[60]

Within weeks, a spokesman for the California Department of Public Works announced that use of the name Mammoth Pass Road would be changed to Minaret Summit Road. Soon afterward, the Bureau of Public Roads notified the California Division of Highways that its new designation would be Minaret Summit National Forest Highway. There was no shortage of agencies wanting to remain involved with a new trans-Sierra thoroughfare.[61]

Sisk, as a federal legislator, knew the key to success was finding adequate funding. Not fooled by prior lowball construction estimates and with twenty million dollars as his own best guess for a completed highway, he focused on three possible sources, all of them federal: USFS budget for improving forest highways, similar appropriations in the NPS budget, and major federal grants. By major he meant the unprecedented nine-to-one matching grants provided by the Interstate Highway Act. Enacted eight years earlier, the program was already a huge success in terms of road miles completed or currently under construction. Sisk carefully downplayed the prospect of another interstate crossing the Sierra Nevada, an image that would surely galvanize his opposition. Instead, he just referred to major grants then quickly pointed to the longstanding corridor provided for just such a road he believed necessary for his constituents. The Minaret Summit Highway, as he now referred to it, would save Central Californians the enormous expense of always having to take the long way around to all points east."[62]

Two months later, Sisk announced from his Capitol office that "all agencies" were in support of the Minaret Summit Road proposal. Omitting named sources, he included the Federal Bureau of Roads, USFS, NPS, and State of California. A reporter for the McClatchy Newspaper Service quoted one unnamed source who mocked that it would take forty years to secure funding for such a road, diminishing somewhat the impact of the congressman's statement. Undeterred, Sisk urged his fellow Central Valley legislators to take necessary first steps with state highway authorities.[63]

Within three months, the efficient congressman had affirmed his own position on the road, identified the important players, determined possible funding sources, and pinpointed the principal barrier to progress: a missing state highway designation. Ever since federal road subsidies were first appropriated in the 1920s, local governments held responsibility for all maintenance. Even for projects as large as interstate highways, all servicing after

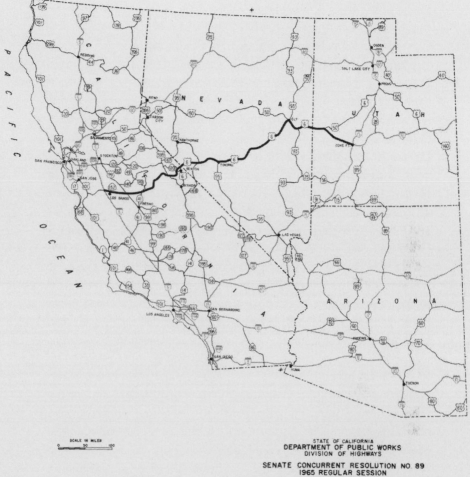

STATE OF CALIFORNIA
DEPARTMENT OF PUBLIC WORKS
DIVISION OF HIGHWAYS

SENATE CONCURRENT RESOLUTION NO. 89
1965 REGULAR SESSION

STUDY OF
TRANS-SIERRA ROUTE VIA MINARET SUMMIT
INTERSTATE 5 TO NEVADA STATE LINE

REGIONAL MAP

MARCH 1966

Congressman Sisk envisioned the extension of I-70 from Utah across
the Sierra Nevada to San Jose, CA.

CREDIT: *Caltrans Highway Report, copyright 1965*

completion remained a local obligation. State highway designation was therefore a prerequisite; the battle for the road had to be fought first in Sacramento.

While advocates knew they had a powerful new ally in Congressman Sisk, opponents were grateful for the support of Judge Raymond J. Sherwin. Appointed to the Superior Court of Solano County immediately west of Sacramento, Sherwin could rightfully claim a longstanding Eastern Sierra heritage. His great-grandfather had constructed the first Sherwin Grade rising out of Bishop, California, the gateway to Mammoth Lakes and communities beyond. Judge Sherwin's elders had first settled at Mammoth Camp. He owned a cabin off Old Mammoth Road and was a frequent all-season visitor. Even though Congressman Sisk had demonstrated geographic awareness uncommon among road advocates, he could never match the judge's familiarity with the Sierra Nevada. Sherwin had systematically explored every mile of the designated corridor, especially its undeveloped gap between Red's Meadow and Clover Meadow. Few if any parties involved in the controversy could claim equivalent topographical understanding.[64]

Judges often conduct their own pretrial inquiries, so it was a simple matter for Sherwin to pick up the phone and gain entry to the highest levels of legislative bureaucracy. He was familiar enough with Sacramento politics to keep tabs on each one of the road initiatives in play. Furthermore, he was practiced in the composition of carefully argued opinions, all based on factual evidence and thoughtful interpretation.

The first of his many discourses on the road issue appeared in February 1963 in the form of a "Mammoth Pass Road Newsletter." He knew very well that a road would never cross Mammoth Pass, but he was writing for the understanding of both factions, and in 1963, the road advocates only knew of a "Mammoth Pass Road." "Nobody over there [the west side] really knows anything about the geography," Judge Sherwin often said.[65]

In his newsletter, he cited money as the biggest obstacle facing the road campaign. Reviewing the proposal's history, the only forward movements came with application of meager budgets available only for repair of forest roads. Sherwin called attention to contradictory actions taken by the various agencies involved, summarizing them in a style typical of a judicial opinion:

> THE RECORD INDICATES that although California's Highway Commission and Division of Highways disavowed responsibility, it was their decision, made in 1960, prior to any public hearing on the merits, upon which the Federal Bureau of Public Roads and U. S. Forest Service based the inclusion of the Mammoth Pass Road in the Federal-Aid Highway and Forest Highway Systems once feasibility was established. No explanation for the Commission's doing what its members previously represented they could not do appears in the applicable California Law.

REALIZING THE PROJECT had at one time been declared "feasible," whatever that meant, he still believed it was a road without any actionable funding source. Nonetheless, arguments pro and con needed to be heard in a public forum, so in his newsletter he offered counterarguments to some of the advocates' claims:

1. That the road was important for national defense had been refuted by the California Civil Defense Director and no less an authority than General George C. Marshall, former Army chief of staff and coincidentally a fisherman familiar with the grandeur of the High Sierra.
2. That the road was needed for continuing timber harvest had been denied by regional forester Charles Connaughton.
3. That the road was important for access to iron ore and tungsten along the Ritter-Minaret Crest had been adequately deprecated by subsequent explorations.
4. That a closer link to transcontinental routes for trucking produce could help the San Joaquin Valley was fallacious; large rigs could make better time over Donner Summit using I-80.

HAVING DISPOSED OF the principal economic arguments, Sherwin summarized various official positions to the extent he could identify them at the time. "Proponents," as he liked to call his adversaries, held the clear advantage for making their position known to the many agencies involved. Sherwin agreed with highway commissioner Christopher Warlow that the Sierra Club, often changing its position, had bargained away its privilege to oppose the road. The judge was amused by the Mono County Chamber of Commerce's announced support of an all-weather road but only if no demands were placed on local budgets. Cost of snow clearance was always a deal breaker. Sherwin had determined the cost of keeping five miles open between Mammoth Lakes Village and the ski area at $1,524 in 1950–51 growing to $18,967 in 1957–58. It didn't take a genius to calculate the expense of keeping a road cleared across the entire range.

One argument he found interesting was the claim that by restricting transportation access, many people would be excluded from enjoying the beauty of the mountains. Sherwin's response went like this: "The entire Sierra Nevada is more than four hundred miles long and at least seventy wide. Of this only a narrow strip remains wild; all the rest is easily available to motor travelers walking a half day from their vehicles. Furthermore, road builders cannot have their cake and eat it too. Once a road comes in, the wilderness is lost for *all* time."

Despite the judge's command of the facts and impeccable logic, the fight was by no means over. Confrontations at city and town council meetings had been mere skirmishes compared with battles to come in Sacramento. Meanwhile, road advocates must have known by then that they faced a formidable opponent in Judge Sherwin. Certainly Sherwin understood, as did his well-positioned partner, Ike Livermore, that they had an imposing adversary in Congressman Sisk, who could summon the power of the federal purse.

HIGHWAYS OF HISTORY

"Oh public road, you express me better
than I can express myself."
Walt Whitman, "Song of the Open Road"

T HE PROPOSITION THAT trails frequented by wilderness creatures were the antecedents of native overland trade routes, or of wagon roads, or of railroad rights-of-way is a false notion of transportation history. On the plains and in the forests, mankind has long served as the dominant predator whose quarry adopted less vulnerable routes. The demands of wheeled transport required a specific topography, and with the coming of steam power, engineers responded with a new set of functional requirements. Any appraisal of transportation history must then take into account precedent and purpose, terrain and technology.[66]

Always the traveler, man has for most of his time on Earth led a nomadic life, retracing familiar routes in search of food as well as seeking protection from the elements. Following the introduction of cultivation and resulting crop yields far in excess of any individual's need, highways were needed for commercial transport. Monarchs also needed roads to move their armies in defense of lands producing the bounty. Throughout history, a ruling elite has largely determined whether a road is built, where it is placed, and how it is to be used. In Mesopotamia, Hammurabi provided a "Camino Real" (King's Highway) for the chariots of his emissaries so they might cover distances of one hundred miles inside of eight hours. In modern society, elected officials and their appointed agents usually control decisions about the funding, construction, and use of highways.[67]

The roads of ancient civilizations were designed and built for immediate use rather than for achieving optimum surfaces, although standards did improve as traffic density increased. The longest road system of antiquity, built by Incan rulers, extended for three thousand miles from modern-day Ecuador to Chile. The upper "Royal Road" was linked by paths to the lower utilitarian coastal road like the rungs of a ladder. Because the Incas never conceived of a wheel, their roads incorporated stairways and rope bridges. Lacking horses and oxen, they relied on the sure-footed llama as their sole beast of burden.[68]

The Romans first surfaced their roads with interlocking stones. Sidewalks were added for the safety of pedestrians at risk from speeding chariots. A ruler's zeal for empire dictated the extent of road-building networks, thus assuring his armies' domination of foreign lands. Ordinary citizens, especially merchants, were sometimes granted access to the roads built by Roman engineers.[69]

The Silk Road, named by history for one of the most desired commodities carried from China overland to Europe, was rarely if ever praised for its surface standards, nor was it a single route but instead a shifting labyrinth of paths, coursing east and west in latitudes as far north as the Siberian border and as far south as the Khyber Pass between what is now Afghanistan and Pakistan. Which route was in use at a given time was influenced by political and military considerations. Whether Marco Polo's accounts of his far-ranging travels were authentic or in part apocryphal, the thoroughness of his diaries was exceptional for those times. Most tradesmen on the Silk Road functioned as middlemen within a limited geographic range, passing on goods intended for distant markets, with generous profit but also with risk of theft.[70]

For centuries, countless chained prisoners proceeded eastward into exile and despair along the Sibirskii Trakt (Siberian Road), a thoroughfare that also saw the movement of armies, the passing of imperial couriers bound for Xian and Peking, and myriad runaway serfs and gypsies. From the opposite direction came tea wagons by the thousands, transporting the precious leaves across the Siberian Steppe to the cities of Tsarist Russia and beyond.[71]

As Europe entered its Dark Age, the magnificent roads built by the invading Romans gradually fell into disrepair. Highway maintenance always requires a strong central authority, and feudal society was at that time decentralized. Until the seventeenth century, roads used for conveyance of armies and trade goods bore little resemblance to their Roman antecedents. The Swiss were noted for their log reinforced (corduroy) roads. But for the most part, roads throughout Europe were deeply rutted tracks, covered with dust in summer and mud or ice during inclement seasons. Not even kings or members of court could find alternatives to substandard conditions. Louis XIV recorded that nine days' hard travel from Versailles brought him only as far as Bayonne; another two weeks were required to reach Madrid. Such incivilities led to the building of toll roads with fees collected in return for easier passage and better maintenance.[72]

Turnpikes, named for the gate that permitted entry, were often financed by a trust. The first of these between London and York was backed by private investors for a twenty-year period, then transferred to local government control. Travel from Bath to London was reduced from fifty hours to sixteen, justifying the cost despite risk of highwaymen relieving wealthy travelers of their valuables as well as opportunities for collectors to embezzle toll revenue.[73]

Not until the nineteenth century would there be sufficient capital for investment in a reliable road network. Napoleon Bonaparte was an early visionary who recognized the importance of upgraded highways for deployment of his troops and conveyance of the heavy artillery required for victory. Because his military strategy depended on a rapid mobile force, Napoleon spent more on highways than he did on fixed fortifications.[74]

LONG BEFORE COLONISTS in North America declared their independence from a despotic monarchy, kings mandated that a suitable road be maintained for the safe delivery of mail between New York City and Boston. On January 22, 1673, Connecticut's governor Francis Lovelace dispatched the first regular mail carrier along the "King's Best Highway." The Boston Post Road, as it later came to be known, was actually two highways, a northern route via Hartford, Connecticut, and Springfield, Massachusetts, and a southern route via Providence, Rhode Island, and New Haven, Connecticut. Its evolution from muddy path to corduroy and finally to crushed stone required additional years. The ingenuity of John Loudon McAdam yielded the "macadam method," loose rock infused with tar producing a surface more friendly to bicycle and automobile tires alike.[75]

Transportation in America captured the fancy of its founding fathers. Even before Thomas Jefferson dispatched Lewis and Clark to explore the far northwest, he had conceived a network of canals and highways to encourage migration westward. During his travels throughout America in 1830, French journalist Alexis de Tocqueville reported that "Americans are at ease only in their restlessness." At the time, twelve thousand miles of wagon roads existed throughout thirteen states, their maintenance the job of each township along the way.[76]

Although government was expected to participate in the cost of a transportation network, events didn't always work out that way. An Indian trail extending westward out of Baltimore was widened to twelve feet by British Gen. William Braddock but abandoned after the French and Indian War. Later resurrected as the "National Road," Congress never granted the funding necessary for grand purposes imagined for project. An attempt in 1806 to extend this road over Maryland's Cumberland Gap was postponed until 1811 and then delayed by war with England. Not until 1818 did a right-of-way extend as far as Wheeling, West Virginia, the first road in America with engineering standards for width (66 feet) and maximum grade (8.75 percent). The National Road, later designated US 40, eventually reached Columbus, Ohio, at which point federal subsidies terminated and individual states assumed responsibility for maintenance.[77]

British precedent for privately capitalized canals and toll roads was fully embraced by entrepreneurs in America. Encouraged by President George Washington, Pennsylvania granted a charter to the Philadelphia and Lancaster Transportation Company. Sixty miles of improved wagon roads were completed at costs averaging five to ten thousand dollars per mile. Tolls were set at "two bits" (twenty-five cents) and collected every six to ten miles. Within a decade, turnpikes were serving travelers between New York City and Boston. Competing toll roads lined both sides of the Hudson River. Meanwhile, New York governor Dewitt Clinton sponsored financing for the Erie Canal. Opening in 1825, "Clinton's Ditch" as it was respectfully and mockingly called eventually secured for New York City commercial dominance over Boston and Philadelphia. Meanwhile, at the canal's western terminus, Buffalo became a major transshipment hub, bringing enormous wealth to that inland city.[78]

In the West, a vast network of wagon roads sprang from the ingenuity of pioneers in search of uninhabited territory. The fabled Santa Fe Trail, for example, facilitated travel from Franklin, Missouri, through Indian lands to Santa Fe, New Mexico, a privilege for which Congress paid the affected tribes thirty thousand dollars. Numerous wagon trails departed Independence, Missouri, bound for Fort Laramie, Wyoming, Salt Lake City, Utah, or Helena, Montana, and destinations beyond. The John Mullan Wagon Road served as an overland route westward from Fort Benton,Montana, where Missouri River navigation terminated, to Walla Walla in what would become Washington state.[79]

Essential for overland transit in 1850 was a robust mule, which cost its owner the same as the sturdiest of wagons: about one hundred dollars. A twenty-mule team, therefore, required an investment of two thousand dollars, more if the risk of replacing lost stock was included. By 1870, the price of a healthy mule had risen to five hundred dollars because supply could never meet nineteenth-century demand. With the advent of railroads, demand for and cost of a mule quickly fell, and all motivation for spending public funds on new roads and their maintenance came to a halt. Between 1849 and 1860, thirty thousand miles of track were laid in America, by 1890, one hundred and sixty thousand, reaching an eventual peak of two hundred and fifty thousand.[80]

Only because of the sudden enormous popularity of bicycles would any stimulus return for improving road conditions. Albert Pope, living as a boy alongside the Boston Post Road, is credited with transforming the high wheel velocipede into a much safer bicycle with two wheels of equal size and pneumatic tires. His ingenuity prompted a cycling frenzy in the 1880s. Soon after this people were attaching electric and later gasoline-driven motors to the rear wheel drive. Pope's Columbia Bicycle Works in Hartford, Connecticut, later became the Columbia Automobile Company. Pope's astounding financial success allowed him time to lobby for surface improvements along the Boston Post Road.[81]

On display at expositions in Chicago (1893) and Buffalo (1901) were the latest in carriages and bicycles, but at the Saint Louis World's Fair (1904), 140 automobile companies exhibited their products. Traveling across the continent in 1903 required four days by rail and sixty days by automobile if accompanied by a mechanic. Railroads remained the workhorse of both commerce and private travel. The automobile was considered a pleasure vehicle for the privileged classes. Henry Ford changed all this by making the Model T affordable to his own workers. The manufacturing center for engine-powered vehicles soon shifted from Hartford to Detroit, Michigan.[82]

By 1921, 2.3 million registered automobiles were driven on three million miles of roads. Twenty years later, population had grown by 70 percent, and eighty million automobiles were using the same three million miles of drivable highway (not including urban streets). During that interval, highway development had become the responsibility of local governments, and the commitment to road improvements varied widely from one political district to the next.[83]

California demonstrated its early support of road travel. The first licensable automobile was registered in 1896, the same year a Bureau of Highways was established. The first road designated as a highway, today a segment of US 50, extended from Placerville, California, in the Sierra foothills eastward to the Nevada border.

Licensed automobiles proliferated from six thousand in 1906 to three hundred thousand ten years later. Californians attending their State Fair in 1916 could visit a display of new "high speed" road technology: cement poured over sand and gravel between expansion joints designed to accommodate extreme weather conditions.[84]

More influential than governments were the motorist associations, which provided the incentive for more than 250 special highways; for example, there were the Theodore Roosevelt Highway in Maine, the Yellowstone Trail, the Pikes Peak Highway, and the Old Spanish Trail from St. Augustine, Florida, to San Diego, California. Firestone executive and highway booster Carl Fisher generously supported the Lincoln Highway Association whose goal was a coast-to-coast highway from New York City's Times Square to San Francisco, crossing Donner Summit on the way, a remarkable engineering achievement for that era. Active lobbying by the highway associations led to state legislation that imposed the first taxes on fuel, beginning in Oregon where the popular slogan was "Help lift Oregon out of the mud." By 1932, when Congress placed its own penny tax on gasoline, every state in the union had adopted fuel taxes.[85]

The nation's military leaders weighed in with their own opinions about the sorry status of roads in America. In 1919, a young officer named Dwight David "Ike" Eisenhower led the first transcontinental army convoy, a post–World War I training exercise. He would later recall the experience as "traveling through darkest America with truck and tank." Departing from in front of the White House, seventy-two vehicles carried thirty-five officers and 260 enlisted men westward. After sixty-two days and nineteen hundred vehicle breakdowns, the convoy reached California where Ike declared its roads the best of the entire journey. Summarizing the exercise, Gen. John Pershing left no doubts about the nation needing a better highway system.

One outcome of Pershing's plea was a system for numbering major highways. The Federal Highway Act of 1921 assigned even numbers for east-west roads and odd numbers for north-south routes. The Boston Post Road and its southern extension became US 1, the Pacific Coast Highway, US 101.[86]

There were diagonal roads as well, the most famous being US 66, the Will Rogers Highway, which extended from Michigan Avenue in Chicago into America's heartland; around the southern end of the Rockies; across the Colorado Plateau, New Mexico, and Arizona; through the Mojave Desert before descending El Cajon Pass into the Los Angeles basin; and terminating at Coast Boulevard in Santa Monica. In his 1939 classic *Grapes of Wrath*, John Steinbeck referred to Route 66 as "the mother road, the road of flight, a long concrete path across the country, crossing the divide and then down into the terrible desert," because thousands of Dust Bowl emigrants depended on it for economic salvation. Later it served as a year-round favorite of tourists and truckers alike because it enjoyed the fairest weather and the least grade challenges of any highway in America. Decommissioned in 1977 after a half-century of colorful history, the nation's only iconic highway with its own musical theme—"get your kicks on Route 66"—could no longer compete with the interstate highways.[87]

After replacing colorful highway names with designated numbers, the federal government ended popular support from groups like the Lincoln Highway Association, whose namesake thoroughfare now became US 40 from coast to coast. Congress became responsible for all major highway development and negotiated with local governments for maintenance. The first Federal Aid Highway Act of 1916 had limited its subsidy to rural post roads, eliciting protests from truckers who knew all highways were worn out. Sequel legislation in 1921 was massive by comparison, providing seventy-five million dollars in one-to-one matching funds for states prepared to invest in major road development. Subsidies were added for building forest roads in the national forests and parks. Both the Hoover and Roosevelt administrations kept federal highway support alive, increasing paved mileage from three hundred eighty-seven thousand miles in 1921 to more than one million miles in 1941. Following the Japanese attack on Pearl Harbor, however, transportation subsidies were entirely devoted to the railroads until victory came in 1945.[88]

By the end of the war, the nation heard once again from its returning military leaders, especially General Eisenhower, who had never forgotten his 1919 convoy experience. The role Hitler's autobahns played in Germany's war-making efficiency was vivid in his mind. Eisenhower believed the United States needed a comparable network for its own defense. Americans with automobiles were driving the same shoddy highways available to them in the 1930s, except there were many more vehicles. The only exceptions were the Pennsylvania Turnpike, Connecticut's network of parkways, and California's first limited access superhighway, the six-mile Arroyo Seco Parkway, later to become a segment of the Pasadena Freeway.[89]

When Americans elected Eisenhower as president in 1952, they were buying automobiles and 'hitting the road" in great numbers. A national highway system was near the top of Ike's legislative agenda. He praised California for inaugurating its own ten-year program to improve fourteen thousand miles of state highways and keep them free of tolls. Both New York and Connecticut were coordinating construction of divided parkways out of the city and parallel to the Boston Post Road. Remembering that Franklin Delano Roosevelt had won approval for a thirty-nine thousand–mile highway system but failed to win the necessary appropriations, Eisenhower began his push for congressional action. Estimates for the network Eisenhower had in mind ran as high as one hundred billion dollars. Neither bond issues nor tolls were acceptable to Congress. Exploiting Cold War fears to garner public support, Eisenhower persisted. "The nation needs a highway system that can meet the demands of natural catastrophe as well as defense should atomic war come," he pleaded. "Americans deserve safer highways," he added, asserting that thirty-eight thousand highway deaths in 1955 were preventable.[90]

Success came in 1956 with creation of the "Highway Trust Fund" and sharply increased fuel taxes. The initial appropriation was twenty-five billion dollars, half again as much as the seventeen billion dollars designated for the Marshall Plan in 1947, and at the time, the most expensive public works program in American history. Nearly every segment of major industry participated: steel, coal, petroleum, automobiles, and others. Remarkably, the system's design was fashioned in state capitals, not in Washington.

Defense considerations dictated several construction parameters. Lanes had to be wide enough to permit emergency landing of military aircraft. Therefore, one mile in twenty had to be straight and flat. Bridge and overpass dimensions must allow for passage of the heaviest military equipment. Entrance and exit design had to comply with a national standard. Service station and other commercial venues were permitted only near intersecting thoroughfares.

Missouri became the first state to apply for and receive a 90 percent subsidy to be added to its 10 percent investment. At completion, there were 46, 876 miles of limited access highway requiring 55,512 bridges and 14,756 interchanges. The final cost was $70 billion ($600 billion in today's dollars).

The Interstate System did have its detractors. Social critic Lewis Mumford called it "a rootless, aimless, and disharmonious environment." All plans for dealing with congestion, he believed, were based on the assumption that solutions were simply a matter of highway engineering, not of city and regional planning. The private motorcar held priority over all other means of transportation, public transportation included, no matter the comparative costs. Mumford was equally concerned about the impact of interstate highways on the inner cities. Eisenhower had never imagined interstates penetrating urban centers; Hitler's autobahns had not. But New York City master builder Robert Moses argued for the interstate highways to serve cities, and he won his argument. While the interstates did serve the cities in commercial terms, they also facilitated migration to the suburbs, confirming Mumford's fear that vast zones of urban squalor would be left behind.[91]

Thirty years after the Interstate Act was passed, the Department of Transportation had recorded one trillion ton-miles of cargo moved, a feat accomplished by twenty-one million truckers driving 412 billion miles just on the new highways. But Congress failed to anticipate the impact of interstate highways on the public's leisure habits. A travel boom led to a major expansion of tourism in America. Americans really did hit the road, traveling 2.8 billion miles in 2002 compared with 628 million in 1956.

Commercial establishments along Route 66 and other traditional routes were doomed, while new hotel and restaurant

development along the interstate system served as its own economic stimulus, prompting innovations like the suburban shopping
center. Cultural historians credit the interstates with spawning
such features of American life as fifty-mile commutes, the two-
mile traffic jam, recreational vehicles, the regional mall, and the
spring-break trek to Florida. And as for mortality rates on the interstates: one fatality per one hundred million vehicle miles driv-
en, less than half the death toll recorded for all other US highways.

In the days of the Roman Empire, all roads led to Rome, but
in twentieth-century America, the Dwight D. Eisenhower National System of Interstate Highways symbolized a more democratic
social structure, facilitating an individual's safe passage from one
region to another. Congressman Sisk saw all this happening, in
California and throughout the nation. He was well aware of the
flow of gasoline tax dollars to other districts. It's little surprise then
that he had to have a piece of the federal highway bonanza for his
own district.

"DON'T TELL US ABOUT SNOW!"

MAMMOTH LAKES CHAMBER of Commerce president Chip Van Nattan can't recall when the meeting took place, but he'll never forget one remarkable exchange: "Somebody visiting from Fresno began lecturing us about snow removal, and from the back of the room came a shout: please don't come here telling us about snow!"[92]

A ridiculous notion indeed for anyone to challenge residents of Mammoth Lakes about their handling of snow, something they knew more about than most people. Tons of snow had blown through the passes flanking Mammoth Mountain for as long as anyone could remember. Van Nattan recalled another episode when winter season expertise worked to the political advantage of Eastern Sierrans.

April 18, 1967, was the date set for a public hearing on Assembly Bill 290 (A.B. 290) asking for incorporation of Forest Highway 100 into the state highway system. Making legislators aware of local concerns about the road was important, so Van Nattan and his wife, Beverly, plus Doug Kittredge and Lou Roeser departed for Sacramento, making their way north on US 395 toward mountain passes expected to be open. Snow began to fall, not just an end-of-season flurry, but snow falling with determination. They went past turnoffs for Carson Pass and Echo Summit, figuring that I-80 out of Reno would surely be open given the commercial demand for its use. But as they gained altitude they found themselves in a blizzard with diminishing visibility. Just short of Donner Summit they were stopped by the California Highway Patrol and asked to turn back; the highway ahead was closed. Commercial truckers had already been called off the highway, and their rigs lined the shoulders in both directions.

All four jumped out of their 1957 Ford and engaged the officers. They were from Mammoth Lakes, their chains were installed, and they were experienced with blizzards. Furthermore, they had to get to Sacramento to testify against another highway crossing the Sierra. That earned the attention of officers, who let them proceed but with a warning not to expect evacuation services. Lou Roeser remembers that drive as if it happened yesterday. Atypical for a late storm, the snow was more like the powder that graces Utah's ski slopes, not the moisture laden "Sierra cement" that usually blankets California's mountains. As snow accumulated, they stopped, jumped out, cleared their windshield, and drove on until forced to stop again. Descending below the snow line, their visibility suddenly improved. Waiting for them in Sacramento were Dorothy and Lou Fitzhugh, hot food, and a place to unroll their sleeping bags. Dorothy had been aware of highway closures and was taking notes from her files in case she was the only road warrior available to testify. A knock on the door had brought her reassurance. The next morning they all proceeded to Sacramento.

The group arrived at the legislative offices early to lobby key committee members, of whom not many had read anything about the bill before them, not even the crucial highway report. In the hearing room, they greeted allies. Judge Sherwin was there and so was Genny Smith. She came toting a giant poster that portrayed the road issue in graphic terms. Eastern Sierrans believed they were ready for battle.

THE LEGISLATIVE DRIVE for A.B. 290 had kicked off two years before with the June 1965 submission of Senate Joint Resolution 89. Resolutions serve the purpose of instructing agencies about legislative directives, in this case asking for a Division of Highways feasibility study. A resolution commits no more expense than the cost of the inquiry itself. The reason for this study went beyond placing a forest highway into the state's highway system; also up for consideration was incorporation of the right-of-way into the interstate program. Sponsors of the legislation were clearly receiving guidance from Congressman Sisk.[93]

While completion of the highway study was awaited, local jurisdictions had weighed in on the issue. Lone Pine's Chamber of Commerce decided it would fight a decision on the Minaret Pass Road until the forgotten Haiwee Pass road from Porterville to Lone Pine was resolved. By appearing to support a hopeless project, they were demonstrating resistance to further road building of any kind. Meanwhile the Mono County Board of Supervisors reversed a prior position, voting to include the Minaret Summit Road in the highway system. They had apparently forgotten that residents of Bridgeport, the county seat, were outspoken in their preference for upgrading the nearby Sonora Pass road rather than committing tax revenue to an entirely new trans-Sierra highway.

Meanwhile Ike Livermore, who kept watch for any initiatives that might advance the Minaret Summit Road issue, received a reply from his letter to the USFS asking for revisions in certain primitive area boundaries. Livermore wanted nothing less than elimination of the corridor, but in his letter, Forest Supervisor Walter Puhn explained that recent revisions were limited to preserving authentic wilderness while retaining the corridor which he considered less interesting terrain. He went on to restate USFS policy, which took no official position for or against the road. Should it be built, he added, he was confident it would cross only granite and dense timber, implying that wilderness terrain could be effectively partitioned into appealing and nonappealing sectors. Livermore was appalled. At least he knew the USFS was not about to relinquish its fence-sitting position.[94]

For road activists and warriors alike, 1966 would be remembered as the year of the highway report, two reports actually. The first was so devastating for the road advocates that supplementary study with revised parameters was demanded. The first was issued

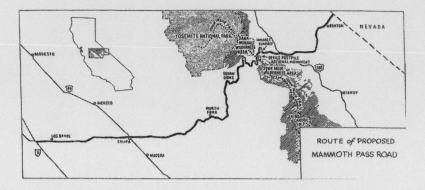

CREDIT: *Caltrans Highway Report, copyright 1965*

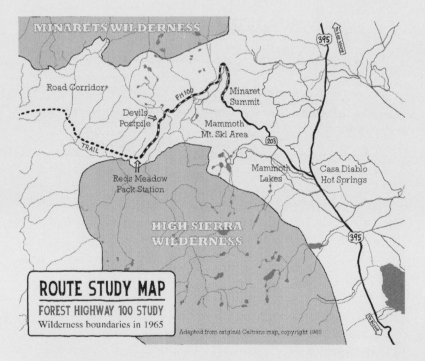

CREDIT: *Caltrans Highway Report, copyright 1965*

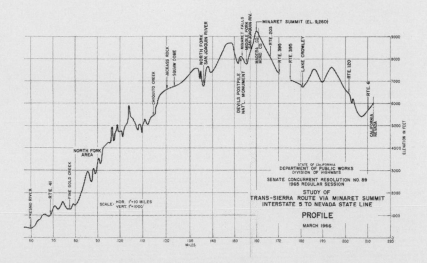

CREDIT: *Caltrans Highway Report, copyright 1965*

in March 1966, the second in December, but their findings, conclusions, and recommendations remained unchanged. Although these pivotal reports didn't bring an end to the road campaign, they imposed a lasting impact on all future debates.[95]

Whereas the last feasibility survey had been completed by the Bureau of Public Roads (BPR), a federal agency, this study was conducted by the California Division of Highways, responsible for establishing budget priorities, letting contracts, and providing all maintenance including snow removal when required. Its conclusion could not have been stated more clearly: "that no portion of this proposed route should be added to the state highway system." Furthermore, the agency pointed out that, "owing to the non-availability of additional mileage for the Interstate Highway System, this route should not be recommended as an extension of that system."

In proposing that their road become a part of the interstate network, neither Congressman Sisk nor any other legislator had considered the current status of established commitments. In fact, all forty-one thousand miles authorized by Congress had been allocated to state and county highway districts. California's highway

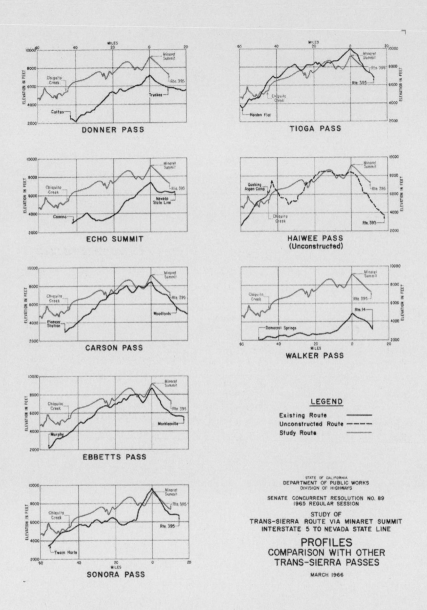

Only on Donner and Echo Summits at much lower altitude is year-round transit possible.

CREDIT: *Caltrans Highway Report, copyright 1965*

engineers knew very well that they had participated fully in the project. The coastal city demand for major highways had prevailed. All projections for an I-70 extending westward from Utah demonstrated low traffic density potential.[96]

The press reacted more quickly than the legislators. A *Bridgeport Chronicle-Union* headline declared the "Minaret Highway Doomed." A more skeptical *Fresno Bee* reported that the findings would be examined. But no matter who was writing about the report, the facts were now in plain sight: cost of construction from CA 99 in the west to US 395 in the east was now estimated at $100 million with additional expense for maintenance including snow removal placed at $6.5 million a year. Just for keeping the road open all year, the price tag read $1.3 million, representing 17 percent of the state's budget for snow clearance.[97]

Mono County Resource Committee members were delighted with the report's conclusions. They had no difficulty understanding the projected budget because they lived the snow removal experience every winter season. They knew why mountain passes higher than 9,000 feet represented a unique challenge. Highway supporters in Fresno and Madera Counties were less accepting of the report's substance. "We want this road," declared a council spokesman, vowing to battle on and "get the highway built no matter the opposition."[98]

Six days after the highway report was issued, Congressman Sisk announced that he and MSHCC members would be going to Sacramento "to plead for the future welfare of the people of California." He was expecting members of the Committee on Transportation to hear him out, but this was not political landscape that Sisk held power to influence. For new arguments, he turned to Glenn Dorfmeier, chairman of the Sierra Land Use Committee, whose revised position went like this: "The California Highway Planning Division went too far with the scope of their study. We just want a highway built to forest highway standards and not a multi-layered [sic] freeway that the state's study was based on." The delegation was leaving behind Sisk's funding strategy; namely, that the proposal must embrace interstate standards in order to qualify for those major grants.[99]

No matter because their pitch seemed to work. Inside of two months, legislators claiming to plead for all of the people of California introduced yet another initiative: Assembly Concurrent Resolution 44, this time demanding another inquiry, essentially a "restudy of the feasibility study." This time the construction parameters were constrained: a two-lane, forty-miles-per-hour road extending from CA 41 on the west to US 395 on the east, in other words fewer miles and no interstate. Left obscured by the wording was the question of keeping the road open year-round. Anyone familiar with what it took to keep a mountain highway open all year knew that many more lanes than two were required to enforce tire chain controls during winter storms.

California highway engineers weren't fooled by the political posturing. Their second report, a minor revision of the first, was issued on the last day of 1966. Its conclusion remained unchanged. Any state road across the Sierra at that elevation would not meet economic feasibility standards, both for snow removal costs and for traffic density. They knew very well that the state's highway budget was strained; FH 100 would remain outside the highway system.

A few state legislators apparently weren't paying attention. Within a month of the second report, A.B. 290 was introduced by Assemblymen George Zenovich and Ernest Mobely, who were joined by twelve more assemblymen and three state senators. The bill requested that FH 100 become a state responsibility. In the accompanying press release, Zenovich made no reference to the highway department report, its findings, or its conclusions. The bill's wording claimed that thirty-two of the referenced seventy-eight miles were already functioning as paved road, but in fact, most of FH 100 remained a poorly graded single lane road with infrequent pullouts to allow for two-way traffic. Paving was sporadic at best.[100]

Ignoring the Division of Highways hundred million dollar cost projection, Sisk had featured only his prior twenty million dollar estimate. The bill contained no reference to a budget for maintenance or snow removal. Independent of this initiative, on January 2, 1967, the Division of Highways submitted its own request for a BPR federal grant of $1.6 million to upgrade the road down to Reds Meadow. State agencies unwilling to spend its own funds are not averse to seeking federal subsidy for similar purposes. Meanwhile Sisk, Zenovich, and Mobley joined forces at a press conference to promote their seventy-eight-mile project, closing with: "It is not a matter of whether the road will be built but rather when and what type of road it will be."

"What type of road, indeed," pondered Bob Schotz, who was posing sample questions for committee colleagues preparing to fight A.B. 290. "How can they list winter sports as a benefit when there is nothing in their budget for snow removal?" A newly renamed committee was now led by Schotz as president, Chip Van Nattan as vice president, and Marilyn Hayden as treasurer, The "Task Force to Defeat A.B. 290 and Preserve the John Muir Trail," was now backed financially by developer Tom Dempsey. Judge Sherwin insisted on the new name. This was not a time for hiding goals. The committee was out to save the John Muir Trail, nothing less, nothing more. Later shortened to the "John Muir Trail Association," the committee continued to benefit from the enthusiasm of Genny Smith, who functioned both as scribe and chief publicist. Taking hints from people in the public relations trade, she produced and distributed notices under the task force heading, always remembering to type "For Immediate Release" at the top. For every alleged road benefit, she countered with an opposing view, usually based on an overlooked fact. Already prepared for the April 4 hearing, she was grateful to learn of a two-week postponement, which granted her an unexpected opportunity to meet Ike Livermore.

Recently appointed Resources secretary under governor Ronald Reagan, Livermore was scheduled to address the Sierra Club's San Francisco Wilderness Conference on April 8. Smith planned to attend but did not expect the road issue to be the featured subject. His words were like music to her ears: "completion of this road in my opinion would be the greatest tragedy in the Sierra Nevada since Hetch Hetchy," referring to the 1920s damming of a Yosemite Park canyon. The road, he added, "would cut across the John Muir Trail, the very heart and soul of wilderness as an effective concept in California. I say stop that road." The resulting applause was thunderous, according to a *San Francisco Examiner* reporter more accustomed to writing about civil rights than environmental issues. Smith made certain that the reporter spoke to all the right people before leaving to file his story, a front-page feature. Smith thought the timing couldn't be better.

Mono County supervisor Arch Mahan liked to conduct his own political advocacy. Considered one of California's most capable politicians, he served as a supervisor for twenty years without electoral opposition. Willing to make his way to the capital to present Mono County's position, he dispelled the fears of Mammoth locals who regarded him a fence-sitter on the road issue. Mahan had interrupted his education in 1924 to support his father's Consolidated Mining operation near Lake Mary. Keeping twenty miners busy year-round, he was forced to shut down in 1934 following passage of FDR's Gold Reserve Act. For the next twenty-six years he managed Reds Meadow Pack Station, an enterprise that flourished close to the proposed route. Mahan therefore stood to gain financially as did his business protégé, Bob Tanner, who purchased the business from Mahan in 1960. Under Mahan's leadership, the Mono Board of Supervisors had wavered between supporting a seasonal road and opposing a year-round highway, but for April's hearing, he planned to denounce the road in terms that left no doubts about his position. He considered the arguments put forth in support of the road to be mostly invalid; for example, he had long provided pack stock for Iron Mountain prospectors and saw with his own eyes that little ore was ever brought out.[101]

Immediately prior to the hearing, a timely letter was sent to the Transportation Committee Chairman by John Forman, representing the Pacific Intermountain Express. It read in part: "Due to elevation and grade of such a highway, in addition to weather conditions, the motor carrier industry would not be able to use such a highway as a gateway to the East," Forman had blown a hole in one of the principal economic justifications for the road. Seasonal or year-round, two-lane or superhighway, it didn't matter. The road didn't make good business sense if it was useless to a major freight hauler.

Livermore hadn't planned to testify at the hearing, but he made his position clear in a letter sent to each transportation committee member. Judge Sherwin, on the other hand, was intent on testifying in person. Genny Smith planned to keep a record of the deliberations. On the morning of the hearing, she and the judge knocked on the door of every committee member, talked to those available, and left packets of information. Chip Van Nattan's stalwart party did the same. A few legislators hadn't done their homework, but Judge Sherwin believed enough had and were prepared to vote responsibly.

As members of the committee entered the hearing room, they couldn't miss a large poster on the easel standing before them. Genny Smith had enlisted a young architect with graphic art skills. Clearly depicted were the superimposed outlines together with elevations of the formidable I-80 crossing of Donner Summit and the even more daunting route up for consideration that day. Also shown were costs of construction using highway department numbers. There were no other graphics shown, so her poster remained in view until the vote.

Organization and planning paid off for the Eastern Sierrans. Chip Van Nattan spoke for the Mammoth Town Council and Doug Kittredge for the Chamber of Commerce. Lou Roeser defined the road's negative impact on the packing trade. Arch Mahan spoke for the Mono County Board of Supervisors, citing problems with the current proposal and urging consideration of an improved Sonora Pass route. Judge Sherwin focused on the shameful omission of Division of Highways cost estimates, directing the committee's eyes to Smith's poster for proof.

Assemblyman Zenovich tried to counter with Sisk's misleading numbers, but the committee had been staring at the poster all afternoon. Eight members remained for the vote; six were against, one for, and one abstained. Lou Roeser can still picture Zenovich leaping to his feet and shaking his fist: "His face went beet red with anger as he warned that the road issue was not dead, that it would be built, that another bill was forthcoming." Speaking later in a more measured tone, Zenovich told a *Sacramento Bee* reporter that the committee had irresponsibly acted on "the greatest amount of misinformation I have ever seen up there." Threatening first to bring the matter before the committee again, he backed off and warned of a new bill for the next session.[102]

The *Fresno Bee* took the news hard: "Solons Kill Minaret Highway Bill." The *Sacramento Bee* also sided with the road advocates, arguing that committee members had demonstrated their indifference to the needs of Central California.

Zenovich and Mobley, although poorly prepared for the breadth and depth of resistance organized by the Eastern Sierrans, reserved their most scathing criticism for Livermore. Representative Sisk joined them in assailing the Resources secretary's involvement and asking whether he was speaking for the governor. Not one of them had expected to have a governor against them who was thought to have once ridiculed trees.

Judge Sherwin summed up the A.B. 290 skirmish best, declaring it "a victory to be sure but everybody needs to keep their powder dry because the battles are not over. Few issues as divisive as this one can be quashed by a single committee vote." Zenovich had already issued his warning: "look for another bill... more likely sooner than later."

ACTS OF CIVIL DISOBEDIENCE

WHAT HAD BEGUN as a pleasant outing quickly became a willful show of defiance. Wives of Mammoth Lakes businessmen, most of them in agreement with their husbands' objection to a superhighway passing through town, decided one autumn day in 1970 to have a look for themselves. Reconnaissance began at Minaret Summit, where construction might have begun. As they walked down the unpaved single-lane road cut into the side of a steep ridge, they were surprised to find surveyors' markers, short wood stakes with yellow streamers attached, placed at sites where more cuts were required for a wider roadbed.[103]

Unaware of any approval to proceed with a survey or any notice of construction, they took the road's destiny into their own hands. Stakes were methodically removed, broken in half, and stuffed flag first into the ground. Everybody pitched in, children included. Before long markers were simply tossed off the downhill slope into the forest below. A smaller party returned the next day to finish the job. One of the crime's perpetrators later admitted the misdeed to her neighbor, Judge Ray Sherwin, and recalled him saying, "I hope I don't have to find a defense attorney for all of you." Sherwin understood that surveying a forest highway under government contract meant their vandalism would be considered a federal offense.

Fortunately, the Federal Bureau of Investigation was never heard from, and nothing came of the incident other than a Bureau of Public Roads notice announcing that because of roadside vandalism, a planned solicitation of construction bids could not proceed as planned. Soon after, an early snowfall effectively buried the crime scene. Little more could be accomplished that year, and there is no evidence the road was ever resurveyed.

Mammoth Lakes author Genny Smith later referred to this episode as "a necessary act of civil disobedience." Marye Roeser, on the other hand, recalled locals believing the road issue had been resolved at the state level, so the agencies were surely acting beyond their authority. In any event, their fun pulling out stakes was a clear demonstration of local sentiment against bringing a high-speed commercial thoroughfare through a community devoted to the enjoyment of a nearby wilderness.

Locals had good reason to believe that the road issue had been set aside. A.B. 290 had been soundly defeated in committee in April 1967, a big victory according to Judge Sherwin and one that was well-deserved by the Eastern Sierrans, who had worked hard and fought smart. But the judge had warned that votes are easily reversed by new legislative initiatives. And that is exactly what happened. Road opponents would have another road bill to deal with by March 1968.

MEANWHILE, NOBODY WAS resting on laurels following the defeat of A.B. 290. Ike Livermore and Ray Sherwin established the habit of communicating frequently by phone and letter. This would continue for another decade. As past directors of the Sierra Club, they knew the organization was diffusely committed and therefore less effective against a chronic issue like the Minaret Summit Road. Both agreed that the political process required advocates to function with a clearly stated objective. So they had urged Mono County Resources Committee to reform as the John Muir Trail Association with one issue before it: stopping the road. Judge Sherwin agreed to serve as an officer.[104]

Livermore noticed that nothing had been heard from citizens or political leaders in nearby Bishop, California, whose business enterprises benefited hugely from Mammoth's recreational facilities. Genny Smith added the names of key figures in Inyo County to her mailing list. Writing to his colleague, secretary of public works John Erreca, Livermore asked for copies of every road feasibility study completed for FH 100. Erreca's department had agreed not to oppose forest highway repairs as long as state highway funds weren't placed at risk.[105]

Members of the Assembly's Transportation Committee received letters of praise from Eastern Sierra citizens long after they voted against A.B. 290. Assemblyman Pete Wilson replied to a letter from Doug Kittredge, saying it was rare to receive thanks after taking action on a contentious issue. Wilson was not yet aware of the pivotal role he would later play as US senator when federal action against the corridor was under review.[106]

Working on his own, Judge Sherwin persisted with efforts to defeat the road in ways that went beyond state politics. Like Livermore, he believed that if the 1962 designation of FH 100 was reversed, then arguments for preserving the corridor would become moot. And so he asked for a May or June meeting with regional forester Charles Connaughton in San Francisco. Hadn't the agency already declared the road unnecessary for timber harvest? As it happened, Sherwin didn't think people attending the meeting—Connaughton, Farin, and Womack among them—were even listening to him. Genny Smith, also present, concluded that foresters are disinclined to relinquish control of terrain already within their jurisdiction. Director Farin, known for his sarcasm, later called FH 100 "the most important unconstructed road in California."[107]

Livermore scheduled his own meeting with Connaughton on August 7. Preparing for that conversation, he sought the position of the US Department of the Interior and was referred to Fred Jones, chief of outdoor recreation planning. A friendly reply revealed that Jones had met Livermore years before while visiting packing stations near Lone Pine. He was clearly in favor of preserving wilderness and praised all that Livermore was doing, He was also careful to write on blank paper instead of agency stationery.[108]

Connaughton later brought with him to the capitol Jack Deinema, newly appointed regional forester, along with two forest supervisors, Joe Radel and Walter Puhn from the Inyo and Sierra National Forests. In a memo to file, Livermore summarized the conversation, noting Connaughton's confirmation that road construction remained possible as long as the corridor reserved for it existed. Nonetheless, he believed there was "no need for this road." Deinema wouldn't commit himself to more than staying "open-minded." Livermore invited him to join a fall pack trip that would include other agency representatives plus a few reporters. He called it an onsite inspection of the corridor zone.

Meanwhile, a bold plan was forwarded by Governor Reagan at the prompting of Livermore that offered to resolve a running conflict over the state's redwood forested lands: California would ask the federal government to cede to the state its Devils Postpile National Monument together with the surrounding wilderness

Regional Forester Jack Deinema holds a sign brought to a fieldtrip as a joke; Ike Livermore joins the fun but for him another freeway across the Sierra Nevada was no laughing matter.
CREDIT: *Phil Pister*

including the road corridor; the state would in turn relinquish selected lands for a Redwoods National Park. Instead of solving two
concurrent standoffs, the idea aroused the fury of Congressman
Sisk, who could see only a plot to remove all hope of building the
road he wanted. Three months after the defeat of A.B. 290, Sisk
accused Livermore of a blatant conflict of interest: ownership of a
backcountry pack station.[109]

Livermore knew how to handle Sisk. First he denied any
conflicts of interest and then he offered to sell his pack station
partnership for ten cents on the dollar, adding that he had suffered
only financial losses. Sisk countered with strong objections to a
high state official leading a pack trip for government officials with
PR motives in mind. "Does Livermore now speak for the Department of Transportation?" Sisk inquired. "We think it's time for the
Governor to express himself on the topic."[110]

Not intimidated by Congressman Sisk's barbs, Livermore
went ahead with the pack trip in mid-September, organized to fa-
miliarize Regional Forester Deinema with the precious territory
placed in jeopardy by the road proposal. Phil Pister of California
Department of Fish and Wildlife was asked to secure necessary
provisions, "including the booze... mostly whiskey and gin." A party of twenty-five foresters, conservationists, and state officials departed from Reds Meadow Pack Station bound for the nine-mile
distant Holcomb Lake, famous for its golden trout. *Sacramento Union* political writer and experienced backwoodsman George
Skelton later called it: "Ike Livermore's Wilderness Summit."[111]

In addition to Deinema, the party included John Lindsay,
legislative secretary for the Assembly; Walter Shannon, director
of California Fish and Wildlife; and Edgar Wayburn, Sierra Club
president who recalled for guests that former governor Pat Brown
had organized similar trips, visiting a different wilderness area
each year. Livermore expressed regrets from Governor Reagan,
who could not be present but confirmed his opposition to the road.
Livermore's comments were even more to the point: "The road idea
is ludicrous and cockeyed." As for Jack Deinema, he acknowledged
that he could recognize genuine wilderness when he saw it: "I don't
think there has been anyone in here for the past ten years." On the

road issue, however, he would go no further than to say: " Our present position is that we have no position."[112]

Arch Mahan came along as did his business partner Bob Tanner, who provided the pack and saddle stock. Offering the unambiguous support of the Mono County's board of supervisors, Mahan renewed his own pledge of opposition to the highway. Inyo County confirmed its opposition one month later. Mono County followed up with a resolution urging renewed engineering studies of CA 108 for conversion to an all-weather crossing of Sonora Pass, perhaps aided by a tunnel similar to Colorado's I-70 transit of Independence Pass. Tuolumne County supervisors lent their unexpected support. As a Sierra Foothills county already served by the Ebbetts, Sonora, and Tioga Passes, their opposition to the Minaret Summit Highway and support for improving CA 108 made good sense.[113]

Ike Livermore wrote to Arch Mahan on October 26, thanking him for eliciting widespread resistance from his fellow supervisors. Livermore knew very well how far and wide Mahan's political effectiveness reached. Reflecting on Mahan's role decades later, Bob Tanner cited his stature as an officer and eventually president of the California State Association of Counties. Mahan knew the territory intimately and could explain the problem of severe grades and heavy snowfalls. In time he persuaded a majority of counties to back him in opposing the highway. Whether or not Mahan's prior business enterprise represented a conflict of interest was surely moot by this time.

While Assemblyman Zenovich's threatened reprisal was awaited, a different Eastern Sierra highway initiative came to fruition with little opposition from anybody. S.B. 21 submitted by the highway department itself, offered a revised course for CA 203. Instead of passing through the heart of Mammoth Lakes and continuing up Lake Mary Road, it would henceforth turn right onto Minaret Road heading past the ski area to Minaret Summit. It was the same route that Dave McCoy had kept open with his surplus Army Weasels. It was a change that must have been encouraged by McCoy. Because it would facilitate access to an expanding ski enterprise, there was no opposition from Mammoth Lake's business community. If anyone was paying attention in Fresno or Madera, they should have recognized a change in the highway grid that helped their cause.[114]

A few weeks into the new year, road opponents learned of a stunning defection from their ranks. Ansel Adams, among the first to lend his name to the cause, wrote a rambling letter to Ike Livermore urging capitulation. Citing the Sierra Club's dithering on the matter, he accused Minaret Summit of being the "least important and least interesting pass in the entire Sierra Nevada. If there has to be another road, then why not put it near Mammoth Mountain and be done with it?" Adams saw logic in uniting two roads already reaching from each side. Had such a juncture been allowed years earlier, he added, then "we would have been spared the tragic invasion of the so-called improved road across Yosemite." Making excuses for not replying in more detail to what must have been one of the more disappointing letters of his personal road battle, Secretary Livermore limited himself to reassuring Adams that the Sierra Club's position was firm.[115]

SURELY A MAN of his word, Assemblyman Zenovich chose March 26, 1968, to fulfill his promise, joining with Republican colleague Ernest Mobley to co-sponsor A.B. 1191. The bill was essentially a resubmission of A.B. 290, but with some notably deceptive revisions. Mobley, who was taking his turn as lead author, had excluded reference to any federal link to the existing forest highway. Instead, the proposal was for assigning state highway designation to an ill-defined right of way that existed between current CA 41 on the west side and CA 203 on the east side. The option of a toll for offsetting extra costs was mentioned, not the custom in a state noted for its toll-free superhighways. Once again there was no mention of prior highway department studies or recommendations.[116]

Forewarned by Mobley's office, the *Fresno Bee* announced the bill in its morning edition: "Mobley Will Present Minarets Road Bill." If passed, state highway status would apply to all seventy-eight miles that lay between CA 41 and CA 203, thirty-two miles already paved, seven to be paved by the federal government, and the remaining thirty-nine to be completed by the state. Alert to these events, Livermore and Sherwin conversed by telephone soon after Mobley's bill was reported by the *Sacramento Bee* and agreed that the resources agency should issue the first dissenting statement. He didn't mince words: "Putting this highway into the system would not only be poor conservation but poor economics!"[117]

Anticipating that Mobley and Zenovich would move as quickly as possible, Livermore mobilized every source of information and support he could think of, beginning with the Division of Highways. Would it stand firm on its past convictions? According to director of public works Samuel Nelson, "the facts contained within the 1966 report are still valid, and the primary recommendations remain unchanged." It was good enough for Livermore.[118]

Legislative analysts in the Department of Public Works made quick work of A.B. 1191, issuing their report on April 9, 1968, just fourteen days after the bill's introduction: "a similar bill as A.B. 290 defeated in Committee in 1967." Highlighting a disparity in cost estimates as well as correcting for inflation, they underscored the Division of Highways opinion that the project was "questionable economically and is completely objectionable to conservationists.[119]

Letters by the dozen began arriving on desks of Transportation and Commerce Committee members. Inyo County supervisor Herb London echoed his board's strong objection to the road. A remarkable letter came from Herbert Joseph, chairman of the California Council for Trout Unlimited. His organization would steadfastly oppose any program to build roads in any part of the 1,256,884 acres of USFS designated wilderness land. The anglers had spoken![120]

In response to Judge Ray Sherwin's inquiries of the trucking industry, Charles Bonner of the Bonner Packing Company returned a detailed analysis of raisin crop transport in California. Tracking the yearly movement of two hundred and thirty thousand tons of raisins to market, he emphasized that only seven thousand tons, about 3 percent, left the state by truck. The rest was carried to coastal ports and waiting ships or else by rail to Canada and eastern destinations. As for the trucks, their loading itinerary usually ended in San Jose, from which exodus by way of I-80 over Donner Summit was most efficient. Truckers would need to backtrack in order use a Minaret Summit Highway. This was the kind of detail that Genny Smith savored for use at key moments during legislative hearings.[121]

Mammoth Lakes resort owner and contractor Bob Schotz wanted to fight the road the best way he could but lacked influence in Sacramento. He had long resisted the pleadings of Realtor Arnold Fryling to become a commissioner for the North Mammoth Fire District, but Schotz knew that Fryling was active in the Republican Party and therefore better connected politically. So they made a deal: Fryling would accompany Schotz to Sacramento and open some doors in return for help with the fire district. The only complication was that Fryling was all for the road being built, yet agreed to listen quietly while Schotz offered facts to committee members willing to listen. Pleased with his efforts in Sacramento, Schotz learned on the way home that Fryling had both listened and changed his mind, promising to do all he could to stop the current highway bill and any more that followed.[122]

Immediately prior to the hearing scheduled for April 30, 1968, Livermore issued a statement he wanted committee members to consider: "Speaking to the economic side it is my understanding that the proponents of this road do not even represent the majority of agricultural interests, nor is it my understanding that they speak for the trucking industry. Speaking as a conservationist . . . this road would bisect the John Muir Trail that travels the length of the High Sierra wilderness. In this great state of ours where we have the largest population, the most prosperous and advanced industries, the richest agricultural valley, the highest mountain, the noblest redwoods, the most spectacular and beautiful state and national parks, we should also maintain intact the country's finest wilderness."[123]

Unlike the A.B. 290 hearing that ended with a vote the same day, A.B. 1191 deliberations persisted on and off for three weeks and never reached a vote. Judge Sherwin attended the first and second hearings; Genny Smith was present for the third. They traded notes when it was all over. Democratic cosponsor Zenovich had assigned Republican sponsor Mobley the task of "managing" the bill, which meant buttonholing individual members for votes. Seven affirmatives were required for passage. Testimony began without a quorum present, and Mobley was in constant motion trying to boost attendance. Members appeared annoyed by the testimony; they had heard it all before. Instead of risking a negative vote, Mobley asked repeatedly for postponements and got them. Follow-up hearings covered the same ground. At no time did Mobley believe he held the necessary votes. The legislative grid shows that the bill was "read into the record" on March 26, "referred to committee" on March 28, and "taken from committee without further action" on September 9.[124]

The *Fresno Bee*, of course, followed the deliberations closely. After explaining to its readers that seven votes were required, reporters quoted Mobley after the first day of proceedings: "The votes were not there... so far it is like trying to hold on to a roomful of feathers in a strong wind."[125]

When the debate came to an end without a vote taken, the traditional culprits were invoked: "Solons Defer Mobley Bill and Minaret Summit Highway." Unwilling to accept another defeat, Mobley asked for indefinite delay to provide time for yet another study, but there was no provision for indefinite postponement; six months later A.B.1191 was procedurally dead.[126]

Pondering the erratic conduct of these hearings, Sherwin and Smith recalled that a decade had passed since they had initiated their formal battle against the road. Despite another interim victory, neither one knew how much longer they would have to argue what seemed an entirely rational position.[127]

Other than Mobley's sole reference to another study, no more threats of a follow-up bill were heard. Only the prospect of improving the existing highway over Sonora Pass remained in play. Assemblyman Eugene Chappie introduced H.R. 310, proposing that FH 100 be withdrawn from any further consideration and that the existing road over Sonora Pass be upgraded to an all-weather highway, including a tunnel if necessary. But nothing came of this bill either. [128]

AND SO THE mothers on their fall 1970 outing in Mammoth Lakes were justified in believing that the democratic process had given them back the sanctity of their Sierra landscape. What they had not taken into account was the determination of authorities intent upon replacing what they believed was a hazardous road with one that assured safe passage for rangers and recreational visitors alike. Their persistence led to finding eight hundred thousand dollars for road improvement, half of it from forest highway funds and the other half from established public road appropriations, all of this with as little fanfare as possible. A surveying contract was solicited and awarded, which explained surveyor's markers.[129]

Except for certain acts of civil disobedience, the Minaret Summit Road issue would lay dormant until 1972.

VIII

MAN IN A "WHITE HAT"

L OOKING BACK TWENTY-FIVE years to his participation in "the greatest political photo-op ever," *Los Angeles Times* political columnist George Skelton remembered "a man waving a white hat as he led a pack train into the wilderness." The man was California governor Ronald Reagan, "a right-winger who unexpectedly became the savior of the Sierra." On assignment for the *Sacramento Union*, Skelton was happy to join what Reagan's press office had billed as a Sierra inspection tour but with an important announcement. "Never to be confused with an environmental icon like Teddy Roosevelt," Skelton mused, "the governor was a far cry from James Watt," referring to Reagan's ill-fated presidential choice for Secretary of the Interior.[130]

The event and its meticulous staging was the creation of Reagan's Resources Agency under the direction of Ike Livermore, whose lifelong devotion to the Sierra served as backdrop. Livermore's everlasting regret was that he could not be present to accompany Reagan. At the request of Nixon White House staffers, he was attending a conflicting United Nations Environmental Congress. While Reagan was making environmental history in California, "I was stuck in Stockholm," he lamented years later.

Livermore's appointment as Resources secretary had not been achieved without challenge. In fact, his was one of the more controversial of Reagan's cabinet appointments. The governor's opponents held that Livermore's family heritage was politically suspect. Both his grandfather and his father had traded in timber, and Livermore himself was serving as a financial officer for the Pacific Lumber Company, a firm that harvested redwood. Opponents asked how someone with his background could possibly function objectively on behalf of the state's natural resources?

While he had never run for political office, Livermore at one time competed for a Republican committee assignment and lost. The offer to join Reagan's cabinet came out of the blue; he suspected it was a Pacific Gas and Electric executive who forwarded his name. When interviewed by Reagan aides Tom Reed and Philip

Governor Reagan announces Norman Livermore's appointment as Resources Secretary in 1966.
CREDIT: *David Livermore*

Battaglia, Livermore was asked only one substantive question: Did he know anything about water? Livermore said no. Yet the job was his if he wanted it. "I think they liked me for my Sierra Club background and for my lumbering experience, such as it was."

At his first meeting with Reagan after accepting the job, the governor jumped up, extended his hand, and said, "I want you to know I never said that about the redwoods." Reagan was referring to being misquoted by former governor Pat Brown, his 1966 opponent. What he had actually said at a Wood Products Association meeting was, "If you've looked at a hundred thousand acres of trees... a tree is a tree; how many more do you need to look at?" A campaign aide for Brown reported it as "If you've seen one redwood, you've seen them all," and the media pounced on the twisted wording. Not of his own making, the quip followed Reagan all the way to the White House.[131]

The governor could not have known in advance what a prize he had in Livermore whom he'd encountered only once before in San Francisco. Livermore had sensed political differences between them at the time; for example, he was prochoice whereas Reagan was an outspoken critic of abortion. But they were quickly drawn to one another, both entirely comfortable on horseback, especially when seeking the pleasures of open country. Why shouldn't he work for a man who said his political life was much more interesting than his movie life had ever been. As the governor's "natural resource man," Livermore served longer than any of the original secretaries appointed. Reagan came to appreciate Livermore as a person so well equipped for compromise that he was remembered as "The Man in the Middle." In preparing for his first political assignment, Livermore learned that Reagan was without blemish for abuses to the natural world and was already on record with a clear environmental objective: "a carefully negotiated balance between conservation and private enterprise." This was not a position embraced by the governor's political opponents.[132]

Nancy Reagan believed that her husband perceived nature more intensely than most people. As a boy, he kept a written account of the wildlife he observed on long walks near his Midwestern home. As a young man enrolled in the cavalry reserve, he became a proficient equestrian content finding untouched scenic landscapes on long rides. As an actor whose romanticized view of the West derived from reading all of Zane Gray, he coveted land ownership. As soon as film earnings permitted him the luxury, he invested in an eight-acre horse ranch north of Hollywood. He later parlayed its appreciating value into buying additional acreage in the Santa Monica Mountains north of Los Angeles. Near the end of his term as governor, he consolidated his land holdings and traded up to his favorite acquisition, 688-acre Rancho del Cielo near Santa Barbara, California. Reagan took his stewardship of land seriously; ranch maintenance became an obsession as well as an emotional release for him. "The outside world is gone... as soon as you get in there [his beloved ranch]."[133]

From the outset, Livermore worked in synchrony with the governor, never against him. Because Reagan's familiarity with environmental issues was limited, Livermore realized his value to the governor and took advantage by speaking out at cabinet meetings. On only one subject, billboards (Livermore hated them) did he hold his tongue at the urging of Mike Deaver: "Actually, Reagan likes them."[134]

Despite Livermore's coaching, the governor could never speak appreciatively of the geography north of Sacramento where he believed there were already more trees than people. Repeated misstatements made him seem entirely insensitive to trees, especially redwoods: "I saw them; there is nothing more beautiful about them, just that they are a little higher than the others." And later: "You know these people from the Save-the-Redwood League scare me. Do they think that all redwoods not yet protected in a park will disappear?"

Livermore was willing to look past these flubs, never criticizing his boss to outsiders, always reminding the press of Reagan's exemplary environmental record. To the *San Francisco Chronicle* Livermore wrote, "I cannot recall a single instance where a decision was made by the Governor that was inimical to the philosophy of concern for our natural environment." Livermore always kept his eye on Reagan's goal of seeking a balance between enterprise and environment.[135]

What he eventually brokered with Reagan's support was an exchange of USFS lands for privately held land with precious stands of old-growth redwood forest. The year 1968 saw passage of a compromise bill providing 58,000 acres of land designated for a Redwood National Park, later expanded to 78,000 acres. The Sierra Club agreed with Livermore that it was a huge victory, not only for conservation but also for Reagan's environmental image.[136]

Water, precious but not evenly distributed, had long been a problem for California politicians, and neither Reagan nor Livermore could sidestep the issue. Admitting that he knew little about water policy, Livermore counted among his most satisfying victories putting a stop to the 730-foot Dos Rios Dam, a misguided venture that could have interrupted flow of the Eel River's middle fork, flooded the 14,000-acre Round Valley, and displaced the Yukis, a 9,000-year-old Indian tribe.

For a meeting in Sacramento, Livermore recalled, "bringing to the governor every representative with a dog in the fight including a delegation of Yukis in full native dress. It was the impassioned words of Yuki elder Norman Whipple that visibly moved Reagan almost to tears." Whipple spoke of the lush valley itself, and of the dependable river, what each meant to generations of his people, how federal troops had driven his ancestors into the valley at gunpoint a century before, and how they were about to drive their descendants back out of the valley, all in violation of sacred treaties. Reagan wasted no time saying what was on his mind: "We've broken too many damn treaties," then excused the pun. "Agreements are made to be kept and we should live with them," he added. Everyone realized it was a critical moment for saving Round Valley from submersion and its native inhabitants from another treaty violation.[137]

Reagan was less interested in highways than his predecessor, Democrat Pat Brown, who was regarded as the development governor by critics and supporters alike. Brown was intensely proud of the expanding network of freeways he had supported throughout his administration. Reagan, on the other hand, would repeatedly disappoint California's road construction industry. Even before he learned of Livermore's longstanding contempt for road builders in the Sierra Nevada, Reagan expressed his criticism of the California Highway Commission "for its tendency to go by the rule of the shortest distance between two points regardless of what scenic wonder must in the process be destroyed." On this theme he and Livermore stood united, a determined campaign to challenge any highway proposal that threatened any one of California's natural wonders.[138]

The intense lobbying efforts of Central Valley farmers and their elected officials in support of another trans-Sierra highway was well-known to Reagan. Livermore continued to monitor the evolving positions of the agencies involved. In January 1972, when the *Bridgeport Chronicle-Union* reported a revised forest service position on the Minaret Summit Highway issue, Livermore immediately queried Mammoth District ranger Richard Austin. His reply came from regional forester Doug Leisz, who summarized prior USFS positions on forest roads and made a distinction between developing a trans-Sierra highway and supporting improvements to an existing FH 100.[139]

Livermore thanked Liesz for the summary but challenged him on several points. Did local recreation user needs mean increased automobile traffic that would negatively affect the adjoining wilderness? Livermore, who believed visitors to the Devils Postpile should either use their own legs or hire a mule, already knew the National Park Service wanted a two-lane road for better vehicle access. So he reminded Liesz that Governor Reagan had weighed in on the trans-Sierra highway issue and did not want it, that the Assembly had excluded FH 100 from the state's network, and that any further deliberations at the federal level deserved to be reviewed by the appropriate state agencies, meaning his own Resources office. To his fellow cabinet secretaries he cited a favorite metaphor: "It's the worm in the apple... are we going to watch it go all the way?"[140]

Reminded by the exchange of letters with Liesz that federal stewards of the parks and forests were resolute in their determination to pursue further road development and were unlikely to cease efforts until construction was under way, Livermore decided the only strategy left was to seek backing from higher authority, meaning other federal departments and their cabinet secretaries, perhaps even President Nixon himself, if necessary.[141]

Beginning in March 1972, the exchange of correspondence between Sacramento and Washington intensified, most of it initiated by Livermore. Agencies never before aware of California's most contentious road issue suddenly became involved. So many experts were given the assignment that formation of an interagency task force became necessary. Geographic distance from the problem made the challenge more problematic. Highway engineers more accustomed to making decisions for roads in the Appalachian Mountains experienced difficulty doing the same for the Sierra Nevada. One agency new to the exchange was the Council on Environmental Quality, appointed to serve an advisory role in the White House. Documents returned to Livermore from the council raised new concerns. The American Association of State Highway Officers involves itself with pavement quality issues. Would the project meet AASHO standards at high altitudes? Worrying about a choice of cement was not what Livermore had in mind when he decided to seek higher authority.[142]

What Livermore did hope for was a cabinet-level decision in his favor. But he had to be careful not to offend regional and district officials by going over their heads to the secretaries of agriculture and the interior. So he advised Reagan to approach Department of Transportation (DOT) secretary and former Massachusetts governor John Volpe. Livermore knew Reagan and Volpe were on a first-name basis through participation at meetings of the National Governors Association.

Time was running out. The *Bridgeport Chronicle-Union* had reported on April 28, 1972, that $1.6 million was already appropriated for improving a 2.7-mile segment of FH 100, enough to widen the road from Minaret Summit to Devils Postpile, plus another $790,000 was available for improvements as far as Reds Meadow. A press release from congressman Harold Johnson's office envisioned two lanes of travel at thirty-five miles an hour for five hundred vehicles each day. This was too much traffic for Livermore and too close to the John Muir Trail. He hadn't forgotten his pledge in 1930 to fight road builders with all the power he held.[143]

Volpe's reply didn't arrive in Sacramento until June 8. "Dear Ron," it began cordially, "Thank you for your April 28 and May 30 letters." But his message was not what Reagan or Livermore wanted to hear. Volpe explained that no commitments to road development west of Reds Meadow had been made at the federal level. What the appropriate agencies were insisting on were reasonable improvements to an existing road believed hazardous to the public. He emphasized that the money was coming from a special public lands authorization without any loss to California. Reinforcing his final point, Volpe hand wrote a postscript citing his department's 1972 allocation of one hundred million dollars more for highway development and maintenance in California than it had granted in 1971. In other words, why was Reagan troubling the DOT over an insignificant forest highway improvement project?[144]

Livermore fumed; it wasn't insignificant to Californians. Now, the only person with sufficient power to cancel the funding was the president himself, a move that would countermand the good intentions of three cabinet secretaries. Reagan answered Volpe's disappointing letter the next day using stronger language but the same arguments. Meanwhile, communication directly with the White House had commenced, even as efforts to win over Secretary Volpe continued. On June 14, executive assistant to the governor Edwin Meese forwarded a full dossier that included 1) a critique of a federal environmental impact statement considered flawed by Sacramento reviewers, and 2) a list of objections filed by local and county authorities.[145]

There was no guarantee that President Nixon would be receptive to Reagan's plea. Both were Californians raised by religious mothers and disengaged fathers. They functioned more as rivals than allies throughout the course of a half-century political interaction. Where Nixon was the fervent realist, Reagan was the passionate optimist. Nixon was suspicious of nearly everyone. Reagan was trusting to a fault. Furthermore, they had butted heads over the Republican presidential nomination in 1968, Reagan trying hard but failing to dislodge Nixon from the ticket, and Nixon later rejecting Reagan as his vice-presidential running mate in favor of Maryland governor Spiro Agnew. Although

Nixon is still praised for combining several small government offices into one very influential Environmental Protection Agency, he, like most Republicans, has never been acknowledged as a conservationist.[146]

Both Reagan and Livermore knew they had a well-placed Washington ally in Caspar Weinberger, who served as Reagan's director of finance before becoming a federal trade commissioner. Later, as deputy director of the White House Office of Management and Budget (OMB), he advanced to the directorship where his cost-cutting would win him the nickname "Cap the Knife." An opportunity to cancel a $2.4 million road project offered him yet another chance to earn that label.

Communications with Weinberger were both personal and public. The outcome of their exchange is well-documented. On June 22, Weinberger forwarded his draft of a presidential statement for Reagan's use to John Ehrlichman, assistant to President Nixon for domestic affairs. Appended to the draft were some explanatory notes: a press conference was planned by environmental activists for June 28 to attack Nixon for Secretary Volpe's decision to proceed with road construction. Coached by Livermore, Weinberger presented another possible scenario: namely, Reagan's public reading of a presidential cancellation of funding, thereby celebrating his administration's conservationist stance. With a stroke of his pen, Ehrlichman wrote "no problem" in the margin, indicating his own and the president's approval of Weinberger's words and the intended publicity.[147]

Whether or not they realized it at the time, Reagan and Livermore were fortunate to have distracted the White House from other compelling events taking place. At a press conference that same day, President Nixon uttered his first denial of any connection with a recent burglary: "The White House had no involvement whatever in this particular incident." Two days before that, eighteen and a half minutes of magnetic tape were erased from a recorder in the Oval Office, presumably containing high-level conversations about a June 17 burglary attempt at the Democratic National Headquarters in the Watergate office complex. In time, those events and more to follow would have grave political and personal consequences for the president and many of his staff.[148]

EVEN BEFORE LIVERMORE knew whether his White House pleadings would bear fruit, he proceeded with plans for an event where his boss could take a very public position on the Minaret Summit Highway issue. More than simply canceling a federal road project, his stand would preserve the integrity of a Sierra Nevada wilderness. What Livermore came up with was later characterized by political biographer Lou Cannon as "one of the most successful media events of the Reagan governorship."[149]

Given an opportunity, the governor was always willing to mount a horse and enjoy a ride over scenic terrain. In this case, he would be doubly pleased for another chance to repudiate government power. Livermore knew the perfect site where the objective could be achieved. He wanted the press conference held at Summit Meadow, a majestic viewpoint in the Sierra backcountry. It was close to the historic pack route, which was also the route destined for pavement if another trans-Sierra highway was built. The site was easily accessible out of the Reds Meadow Pack Station where Livermore had first pledged his battle against Sierra road building. Bob Tanner and his former business partner, Arch Mahan, were the perfect hosts for this event. Tanner and his wife, Jean, had done it many times before. "We were not starstruck," she later recalled. "We guided sports figures like Olympian Bob Mathias, myriad corporate executives, military brass, countless Hollywood celebrities including John Wayne, as well as former defense secretary Robert McNamara."[150]

An ambitious invitation list included representatives of several state and federal agencies, including the USFS, NPS, and Caltrans; the Sierra Club and other groups with a stake in preserving the wilderness; and elected officials from every involved county. Of course there would be reporters because it was a press conference. But how many people altogether? For Bob Tanner and his crew, this was a challenge, not knowing in advance exactly how many would attend and what their trail expertise might be: experienced, novice, or green (which meant never on horseback before).

Governor Reagan's wilderness hostess, Jean Tanner, seen here on
Spider K, her prized Leopard Appaloosa
CREDIT: *Jean Tanner*

Tanner preferred a single-day affair, but Livermore wanted the event to span two days. An advance party of fifteen would
include packers and pack stock (mules), provisions, camp gear,
and personal duffle for experienced campers riding saddle stock
(horses). Logistical planning for a longer event required more of
everything: stock, feed for stock, wranglers, cooks, and tents for
protection during inclement weather. The Tanners deferred entirely to their friend Livermore's sense of public spectacle. First learn-
ing about the idea months before, they had to scramble when told
it was happening in one week.

Suddenly faced with accommodating fifty to sixty guests,
including the governor's security detail, Tanner contacted Herb
London at Rock Creek Pack Station for additional stock. On the

afternoon before dignitaries were due, he appealed to Lou Roeser at Mammoth Pack Outfit for more; Lou agreed to bring nine horses plus his sixteen-year-old son Lee for additional wrangling.[151]

On the appointed day, Mono County supervisor Arch Mahan was joined by Dave McCoy at the Minaret Summit Vista, both prepared to greet people as they arrived. For anyone willing to pause and enjoy one of the grandest panoramas in the Sierra Nevada, they offered a geographic orientation. To the north and west, beyond a broad densely forested valley carved by the San Joaquin River, lay the minarets and ragged pinnacles of the great Ritter Range, a favorite of John Muir who called it the most divine of all mountain ranges in the world. To the immediate south loomed Mammoth Mountain with its impressive ski facilities. And to the southwest and beyond the river there were massive ridges of granitic rock, some rising more than 8,000 feet, higher than any existing interstate highway. Only from this perspective could someone appreciate the technical challenge of constructing a modern highway without abusing the terrain.

Some took time to enjoy the vista while others forged ahead, descending 2,000 feet in eight miles on a winding, unpaved 11 percent grade rarely more than a single lane in width. At the three-mile marker a hairpin turn redirected motorists south through a forest of pine and fir, past glimmering lakes, past the Devils Postpile National Monument, and into the pack station where the road abruptly ended. Everyone was happy to be there except for a few reporters representing the major wire services, California's major newspapers, and publications serving the Eastern Sierra. They were all annoyed by omission of the customary advance press release. Some of the press corps knew what was expected of them and looked forward to the adventure, while others were beyond their skill level and wished they had remained in one of Mammoth Lakes' comfortable taverns waiting for the mystery event to unfold. The guest of honor had good reason to withhold his message. It would be revealed in good time but only in the setting carefully chosen for release.[152]

Lee Roeser awoke before dawn on June 28 and set to helping his dad select horses with temperaments suitable for novice riders. Meanwhile, Marye Roeser made certain that all were fed

Lee Roeser at sixteen helped his Dad Lou take Governor Reagan's party on their wilderness ride, June 28, 1972

CREDIT: *Marye Roeser*

adequately, men and stock. She wished she could be present for the action, but since Nancy Reagan wasn't coming, the event was declared, "for the boys only."

The governor and his party departed Sacramento early that morning bound for Mammoth Lakes Airport. Escorted by the California State Police, his motorcade passed through Mammoth Lakes, then up Minaret Road past Mammoth Mountain Ski Area,

Governor Reagan on Lady and ready to depart
CREDIT: *Russ Johnson*

Governor Reagan enjoys a sandwich on the trail along with Arch
Mahan (l), Mono County Supervisor; and Herb London (r), Inyo
County Supervisor
CREDIT: *Russ Johnson*

across Minaret Summit and down into the valley below. Arriving
at the pack station about 9 a.m., Reagan was greeted by hosts Jean
and Bob Tanner, along with Mono County supervisor Arch Mahan
and Inyo County supervisor Herb London. Jean was soon distracted by a security officer's peculiar notion of flanking the governor
with members of his detail.[153]

"But the trail isn't wide enough for that!" she explained.

"We'll be fanned out in the woods on either side of him,"

"But It doesn't work that way here," she insisted. "Mules and
horses are trained to follow one another and to remain on the
trail."[154]

The debate might have continued had not Reagan mount-
ed his horse and announce to Bob Tanner and Arch Mahan that he
was ready to go. Suddenly everyone was scrambling for position on
the trail, including a security detail that ended up well behind the

governor, their rifles held at ready position as if a villain might attack from the surrounding forest at any moment.

Lee Roeser remembers there were five or six horses hand-picked for the VIPs. "The governor had a good one," he recalled, "a mare named Lady." As they all took off, Lee hung back to help the novice riders; he would be doing more of the same along the way. Last out of the gate was hostess Jean Tanner riding Spider K, the prized Leopard Appaloosa she often rode in Rose Bowl Parades. Although the event was supposed to be for the men, she wasn't about to miss out on this backwoods political adventure.[155]

From the pack station, the trail led past Devils Postpile, a rare geologic formation of basaltic columns formed under intense pressure thousands of years before and later polished by glacial erosion. West of the meandering Middle Fork of the San Joaquin River, the party crossed the iconic John Muir Trail and gradually climbed a massive granite ridge to 8,000 feet. Because of a heavy Sierra snowpack that year, icy patches could be seen but the trail was clear of winter accumulation. Dropping down to King Creek at 7,600 feet, they encountered a nearly abandoned campsite where wranglers stood with a string of mules fully packed for a return to Reds Meadow. The advance party minus gear had already moved on to Summit Meadow.[156]

On the far side of King Creek, the trail began its strenuous 1,500-foot ascent, without sun protection although with plenty of ankle-deep and powdery pumice. A few members of the press corps used the occasion of trail switchbacks to dismount, clamber up the slope, and try to engage or photograph the governor. Reagan ignored them all, understanding that the pace of the advancing pack train shouldn't be delayed. Bob Tanner looked down at one point and saw a reporter lose his camera and then lose his own footing at trail's edge. Lee Roeser witnessed the outcome of all the foolishness; his duty was to help reporters remount, not always a simple task for novice riders on a challenging trail. As a result, the pack train was soon spread out for a mile behind the lead mounts.[157]

The reward for all this effort was Summit Meadow itself, a broad expanse used in the past as a pasture for sheep plus a

360-degree view of the surrounding peaks. The first order of business was lunch, served while stragglers rejoined the party. The all-important "kitchen mule" had arrived earlier, laden with two large coolers filled with ice-cold sodas. And there were plenty of cold sandwiches to go around. An easel held for display a regional map with the proposed route marked on it. Viewers could see for themselves how a highway might impact the natural beauty they were experiencing.[158]

Waiting until a satisfactory quorum had gathered, the governor took command of his audience. He was in good spirits after a thrilling ride but also eager to voice the important message he carried with him:

> I HAVE ASKED you to join me today, in this spectacular
> High Sierra setting, to emphasize in the most dramat-
> ic way possible the position we have taken as an ad-
> ministration since 1966 to protect the Minarets from
> environmental harm.

HE SUMMARIZED A longstanding campaign to create another trans-Sierra highway and the matching effort to oppose the project and prevent irreparable harm to the wilderness. Pausing to honor Sierra Club efforts, he continued:

> THE U. S. Forest Service has proposed to spend $2.3
> million to build 2.7 miles of high-speed road to Devils
> Postpile Monument. We have taken strong issue with
> that proposal . . . believe it extravagant and complete-
> ly unnecessary . . . and will provide only a negligible ac-
> cess advantage. Even worse, it would represent a foot
> in the door to those intent on paving yet another road
> across the Sierra . . . in defilement of the wilderness.

NOTHING REALLY NEW to informed listeners up to this point, but he still had a surprise up his sleeve . . . actually deep in his pocket.

> DURING THE PAST several months, we have stepped
> up our fight to keep this from happening. Our efforts
> have not gone unnoticed. Shortly before departing

Sacramento today I received a telegram from the White House detailing the president's complete support of our position.

REACHING INSIDE HIS jeans, he pulled out and slowly unfolded a telegram with a two-paragraph message. Continuing to read from his own statement, he revealed President Nixon's message:

> HE IS ANNOUNCING that the proposed reconstruction of a portion of the Minarets Highway will not be undertaken, and that the proposed trans-Sierra highway will not be built. President Nixon has handed us the victory we have sought for so long. For this action he deserves the thanks of every Californian.[159]

WHETHER UNFOLDING EVENTS in Washington, DC, had delayed the telegram or Reagan was striving for dramatic effect, the impact of his announcement was immediately felt. Although Interior secretary Rogers Morton and Agricultural secretary Earl Butz were already informed of the president's stand, the news had not reached agency representatives in the field. Some minor grumbling was heard at the periphery of the crowd. For purposes of saving face, references to persisting road hazards were quietly voiced. But as soon as President Nixon's position was known, it was no longer politic to mention a trans-Sierra highway.[160]

As the governor finished, he reminded everyone that politics is fleeting, that an elected leader's conviction might not endure beyond his term of office:

> I AM PROPOSING a permanent solution to this problem—to close this corridor forever by merging the existing Minarets and John Muir Wilderness Areas into one. I am convinced that by such action we can prevent the creation of a high-speed trans-Sierra highway through this area for all time and preserve the vast primitive beauty of this wilderness for generations of Californians to come.

THE RIDE BACK to the pack station was less complicated; nobody wanted to place barriers in the path of determined packers and

Governor Reagan reads message from President Nixon reversing decision to fund forest road improvements.
CREDIT:
Russ Johnson

stock aware that their work would soon be over. Given little opportunity for conversation on the trail, Reagan was all for sitting down in the pack station café and talking about horses with Mahan, Tanner, and the Roesers. Reporters interrupted with needling questions about redwoods instead of that day's issue. Nonetheless, "the governor really enjoyed himself that day," Bob Tanner later recalled.

The immediate press reaction was mostly positive. Major newspapers like the *Los Angeles Times* focused on the action taken by the president and not the circumstances of the Sierra adventure. Reporters for local publications, on the other hand, elaborated on the spectacle itself and praised all who planned or conducted it. From the *Fresno Bee* came predictable outrage. Speaking for the Minaret Summit Coordinating Committee, R. W. Atkins had this to say: "We have no intention of lying down and playing dead. Congress has decreed that part of the Sierra not be included in the wilderness area, so it will take more than a president and a governor's order to change it."[161]

Soon after the event, Bob Tanner received word from Madera County tax authorities that he should prepare for an appraisal of his facilities and an audit of recent tax returns. Suspecting retribution for his participation, he wrote and asked whether anyone in the tax office really believed he was powerful enough to stop a highway? No reply was received and the audit never came to pass. Tanner believed it fizzled because the cost of sending a qualified appraiser/auditor team to the pack station far exceeded any possible increase in tax revenue.

REPORTER GEORGE SKELTON, who more often than not wrote critically of the governor, was interviewed by Reagan's biographer Lou Cannon thirty years later and recalled, "It was like the cavalry coming to the rescue." Taking into account the governor's environmental record, Cannon wrote:

> STOPPING THE DOS Rios dam and the trans-Sierra highway would have been monumental achievements for any governor, let alone one who entered office with a reputation as a foe of the environment. That reputation was based almost entirely on Reagan's misguided statements about the redwoods. But Reagan's actions on behalf of the environment during his governorship transcended these words. Governor Reagan saved the wild rivers of the north coast, and he saved the John Muir Trail. It is a valuable legacy."[162]

MEANWHILE, A MAJOR player in the battle for the Sierra Nevada was thousands of miles away. Ike Livermore had long played his relentless role as both catalyst and political operative intent on stopping the Minaret Road Highway by any means possible. For the most recent victory, he displayed his awareness of where political power lay and how best to mobilize it for decisive action.

There was more work to do, however. Governor Reagan was on target: politics is fleeting, terms of office come to an end, and new leaders are often persuaded to lean a different way. The challenge for the present had been met, but the goal for the future was to join the bordering wilderness areas and obliterate the corridor, thereby assuring for all time a sanctuary invulnerable to Livermore's longstanding fear: road builders running wild.

THE IDEA OF A MANAGED WILDERNESS

*"The root of the story lies in the fact that
civilization created wilderness."*
Roderick Frazier Nash, 1967[163]

WHAT DOES IT mean to manage a wilderness by legislative mandate? According to what authority is a wilderness area defined for modern understanding and practical use? And has the idea of wilderness, meaning the public's concept of what a wilderness represents, changed as society has evolved? The answers to these and related questions derive from our own cultural attitudes more than from any benchmarks offered by nature.

What about the word "wilderness" itself? Although a noun, according to common usage it often behaves as an adjective. Commonly used to designate a specific place, the term is also selected to characterize a state of mind. Inherently subjective, any acceptable definition of wilderness can vary from one individual to the next. A visitor from Chicago would likely consider a trip to Northern Minnesota to be a wilderness adventure, but a Yukon trapper might regard the same journey as a return to civilization.

The etymology of the word "wilderness" provides us with little understanding of the question. An Old English term "wildeor" refers to living creatures beyond the control of man. "Wildeor" was later contracted to "wilder" yielding "wildern" and in time "wilderness," meaning a "place of wild beasts." The idea of a habitat preferential to wild creatures implies the absence of man. The resulting image is one of mankind thrust into an unforgiving environment where circumstances for controlling one's fate are limited.

Modern dictionaries define wilderness in terms that portray undeveloped land. Both the prevalence of wild animals and the relative scarcity of man are taken for granted. And whenever the task is to assign the term "wilderness" to any specific site, the difficulty is compounded. How wild must a place be to qualify as a "wildern?" Conversely, how much of civilization must be evacuated to restore a valid wilderness? Dimension presents another dilemma. Wilderness crusader, Robert Marshall, demanded "an area so large it could not be traversed without mechanical means in a single day." Ecologist Aldous "Aldo" Leopold, set a higher standard, a region capable of absorbing a two-week pack trip. And we know that as a college student, Ike Livermore once promoted the idea that a journey into the wilderness should take at least one full day from road access.[164]

The US Forest Service has long struggled to establish a working definition of wilderness. Since the 1920s, its sequential use of words like "natural," "primitive," and "roadless" often created more questions than answers. Even with passage of the Wilderness Act, the operative language remained obscure: "A wilderness is an area untrammeled by man, where man is a visitor who does not remain." The enabling legislation required that a wilderness retain its "primeval character and influence." Untrammeled? Primeval? The problem of meaning lives on.[165]

New World pioneers brought with them an understanding of wilderness that prevailed long before they crossed the Atlantic. Avid readers of the Bible knew of the wild as a land cursed, especially when there was little water for quenching thirst. Plenty of forested land awaited them on this continent, an environment considered both alien and insecure to man. God's received blessing on the other hand usually meant transforming a fearsome wilderness into a land of agricultural bounty.[166]

The land that Mayflower travelers entered was described by their leader, William Bradford, as a "hideous and desolate wilderness." It also represented the necessary source of foliage for protection from the elements and natural foodstuffs for sustenance. Nonetheless, the wilderness represented for white settlers a symbol of mystery and darkness, an attitude not shared by the indigenous people living nearby.[167]

Perhaps no better evidence exists for wilderness being a creation of civilization than the contrast between native and settler attitudes about the land they problematically co-occupied. Chief Standing Bear of the Oglala Sioux explained that his people "did not think of the great open plains, the beautiful rolling hills and the winding streams as being wild, despite their tangled growth. Only to the white man was nature a wilderness and the land infested with wild animals and savage people."[168]

For nomadic hunters and gatherers, the land had been natural and part of an expansive and seamless community. With the advent of agriculture and herding, distinctions were drawn. When pioneers arrived, they fenced fields and corrals, defined towns and townships, and thereby established a more controlled landscape. The white man even brought from Europe the concept of property rights, and so laws were made for protection of land ownership and the banishment of native inhabitants.

When French journalist Alexis de Tocqueville found himself at the "fringes of civilization" in Michigan Territory, he asked to be taken into the primitive forest. Asked why by people who thought him mad, he answered, "For pleasure." In his chronicle *Democracy in America*, he expanded on the point: "In Europe, people talk a great deal about the wilds of America but the Americans themselves never think about them; they are insensible to the wonders of inanimate nature and may be said not to perceive the mighty forests that surround them until they fall beneath the hatchet. Their eyes are fixed on subduing nature... draining swamps, turning the course of rivers, peopling the solitudes."[169]

By the end of the nineteenth century, a new appreciation of the wilderness dawned. Initial gestures toward creation of a romantic wilderness came from literary gentlemen wielding pens, not from anyone who swung an axe. In wilderness, they saw what they wanted to see, not a forbidding land but instead a sublime and welcoming place. These journalists idealized a life far closer to nature than had ever been characteristic of writing in American. New York City–based Fenno Hoffman first popularized the travel essay, sending reports back from the Adirondack Mountains, a landscape that he believed to be an untouched sanctuary ideal for lovers. Charles Lanman, in 1846, described a "wild and silent" wilderness near Lake Superior, "beautiful beyond anything I have imagined."[170]

Reports from official parties dispatched to explore the West were filled with hardships and tales of native belligerence; they also contained superlative descriptions of the terrain. Second Lt. John Fremont's journal of his 1842 journey to Wyoming's Wind River Mountains featured one "grand" or "magnificent" or "romantic" vista after another. His 1843–44 winter crossing of the Sierra Nevada at Carson Pass included these words describing modern Lake Tahoe: "we had a view of a mountain lake at our feet, about fifteen miles in length, and so entirely surrounded by mountains that we could not discover an outlet."[171]

Despite similar sentiments offered by William Cullen Bryant and James Fenimore Cooper, the pioneer disdain for the wild was not seriously challenged until Henry David Thoreau in 1851 delivered his now-venerated lectures at the Concord Lyceum: "I wish to speak a word for nature, for absolute freedom, and for wildness. On this side is the city, on that side the wilderness, and I am ever leaving the city more and more and withdrawing into the wilderness." Americans had not listened to anything like this before. Discarding romantic clichés and coming to grips with a higher reality, Thoreau and his words served as a foundation stone of American transcendental thought.[172]

Whereas the Calvinists recognized a residue of evil in every human heart, transcendentalists like Thoreau and Emerson perceived a spark of divinity, and they believed that their conception of man was complementary to the beauty of wilderness. Although Thoreau was unprecedented in his spiritual devotion to the wilderness, reality eventually proved his expectations unrealistic. Leaving

Concord behind in order to search for the genuine primeval forest in Maine, he was shocked to find "a wilderness even more grim than anticipated." With a respect for civilization somewhat renewed, he revised his message: Ideal man existed in a middle position. "The natural remedy is to be found in the proportion the night bears to the day."[173]

Even as Thoreau continued to lecture and write, the ambiguously perceived wilderness was steadily disappearing from the American scene. Horace Greeley issued a warning in 1851: "I charge you to spare, preserve, and cherish some portion of your primitive forests, for when these are cut away, I apprehend they will not easily be replaced." John James Audubon also noticed the relentless destruction of forests. Francis Parkman, Harvard University historian and author of narrative classics such as *The Oregon Trail*, lamented in 1892 "the wild west is tamed and its savage charms have withered."[174]

It would take more than journalists, poets, romantics, philosophers, historians, and naturalists to bring about a preservation movement with some teeth attached. What it required were men of outspoken conviction like Frederick Law Olmstead; it would also require legislative action. A precedent had been established in 1832 when the Arkansas Hot Springs were set aside as a "national reservation." In 1864, the federal government granted Yosemite Valley to the State of California "for public use, resort, and recreation." Olmstead, one of the nation's leading landscape architects, was familiar with the unique importance of Yosemite and agreed to become a commissioner entrusted with its care.[175]

The first large-scale federal act of public land preservation took place in 1872, when president Ulysses S. Grant designated two million acres in the Wyoming Territory as Yellowstone National Park. In 1885, New York became the first state to preserve a portion of its lands for public purpose: a 715,000-acre tract in the Adirondack Mountains. In Wyoming, advocates were concerned about private exploitation of unique geographic curiosities such as geysers and hot springs. New Yorkers on the other hand were troubled by diminishing water levels in both the Erie Canal and the Hudson River and so reserved the land for restoration of the water table.

What the uninhabited wild places of America still needed was their own champion; they found him in John Muir, a man whose exploration of the wilderness and the praising of its virtues became a way of life. A transplanted Scot raised in Madison, Wisconsin, he left the University of Wisconsin after two years so that he might complete his education in what he called a "University of the Wilderness." When his San Francisco–bound steamer docked in 1868, he asked for the best route out of town. Asked where he was going, he replied, "Anyplace that is wild." He was shown a trail that led him up into the Sierra Nevada. Some believe his spirit has never left those mountains.

Muir devoted many years to exploration but came to realize it was time to attract the attention of people in power, men willing to make lasting decisions about preserving certain sacred tracts of land. The most effective of these was president Theodore Roosevelt, a well-regarded naturalist himself. Muir was willing to postpone a long-planned world tour in 1903 so that he might accept TR's request of his company during a forthcoming Yosemite visit. Roosevelt pronounced that experience "the grandest day of my life." Despite Muir's disdain for the president's passion for hunting, a bond was made.

"Mr. President, when are you going to get past the boyishness of killing things?" he had asked. After a moment of thought Roosevelt agreed with his wilderness companion but never revised his recreational preferences.

Muir sought to persuade the president that Yosemite Valley would be better off if California gave it back to the federal government for union with the adjacent national park. Not only was this achieved in 1906, but two years later a presidential initiative made the Grand Canyon a national monument. Great benefits followed a single overnight experience when four inches of snow fell upon two famous visitors.

Muir wasn't as fortunate when it came to protecting Yosemite National Park's Hetch Hetchy Valley. Those able to recall its natural state, Ike Livermore's father among them, said its grandeur was a match for Yosemite Valley. Efforts to site a dam at the bottom of the valley and create a reservoir for San Francisco were fought for many years. Muir applied full devotion to the task. Roosevelt vacillated. Enormous empathy for the plight of San Francisco following its seismic destruction in 1906 was pivotal. President Taft finally granted his support of the Raker Act, and for the first time and only time so far, an established national park was violated for largely commercial purposes. The O'Shaughnessy Dam was built and the famed Canyon of the Tuolumne River flooded. Muir would thereafter refer to "these temple destroyers, devotees of rampant commercialism . . . who lift their eyes to the Almighty Dollar instead of the God of the Mountains."[176]

Despite the setback, in his lifetime John Muir identified precious lands stretching from the Southwest to Alaska, then taught the American public that these matchless places deserved preservation for posterity. Remembered as the father of the National Park System and of the Sierra Club, his name adorns a mountain, a beach, a monument, and a college, and, most famously, the 211-mile John Muir Trail that runs nearly the length of the Sierra Nevada from Mount Whitney to Yosemite Park.

For Muir, Theodore Roosevelt epitomized the necessary person of power who functioned on a scale far grander than the conservationist ever imagined. The president was able to transfer into public protection more than 230 million acres of national forests, national parks, national monuments, bird reservations, wildlife refuges, waterways, and reclamation projects.[177]

Concurrent with Muir's efforts, Gifford Pinchot was named national forester under the patronage of President Roosevelt, with jurisdiction over the nation's forest reserves. As the first chief of the US Forest Service, Pinchot championed a "wise use" philosophy, or as he preferred to describe it, "the art of producing from the forest whatever it can yield for the service of man." Pinchot coined the term "conservation ethic," but Muir believed him to be a "de-conservationist." For example, Muir disparaged sheep grazing in the High Sierra; "hoofed locusts" he called them. Although the US Army finally drove sheep out of Yosemite Park, grazing was one of the wise uses that Pinchot encouraged.

Pinchot took a decisive stand on the Hetch Hetchy controversy. Like secretary of the Interior James R. Garfield, who said that "domestic use is the highest use to which water and available storage basins can be put," Pinchot agreed and said: "As to my attitude toward the proposed use of Hetch Hetchy by the City of San Francisco . . . I am fully persuaded that . . . the injury . . . by substituting a lake for the present swampy floor of the valley . . . is unimportant compared with the benefits derived from its use as a reservoir."[178]

Pinchot studied in the best forestry schools of France and then at Yale's new forestry management program. So he knew a lot about forests and had attracted the patronage of Roosevelt as early as 1899 in Albany, New York. The forester's preferred style of management was for government to retain land ownership and oversee the forests' many uses rather than subcontract public land and thereby lose control to private companies. A modern version of his "wise use" policy remains in force today.

Government control was not what the Harrimans and Guggenheims and Weyerhausers had in mind; Western lands were too rich in copper, silver, lead and virgin timber to be made inaccessible by legislative decree. Nonetheless, Roosevelt held firm on the land being a part of every American's birthright. And so it fell to the USFS, a new agency formed in 1905, to protect public lands. Its rangers were initially ridiculed as "Teddy's boy scouts," and sometimes even threatened at gunpoint or chased off land assigned to them for safekeeping. Congress, tried to starve the USFS by keeping salaries so low that good people were forced to leave government duty.[179]

Following Muir's death in 1914, new leaders of the conservation movement stepped forward, among them Aldo Leopold, Robert Marshall, Howard Zahniser, and David Brower. New organizations were formed as well, among them The Wilderness Society. Most important of all was an American public newly aware of and responsive to conservation initiatives. The Hetch Hetchy setback was publicized widely, and public sentiment contributed to cancellation of a proposed Echo Park Dam inside of Dinosaur National Monument.

Pinchot was elected Governor of Pennsylvania in 1922 but walked away from politics in the 1930s preferring his role as forester, this time as a voluntary consultant for Teddy Roosevelt's cousin, Franklin. Based on reports and recommendations forwarded to the White House by Pinchot, the Civilian Conservation Corps was launched within the first one hundred days of FDR's presidency, a force of two hundred and twenty-five thousand idle young men put to work in the nation's forests that grew to six hundred and fifty thousand three years later.[180]

In 1949, Wilderness Society director Howard Zahniser revived interest in a wilderness preservation law set aside during the war years. Discussions of a nationwide system of "wilderness belts" parallel to selected mountain ridges had been first held in 1921, and President Franklin Roosevelt always liked the idea. Restored interest produced in 1951 a declaration of intent, a national commitment to safeguarding wilderness areas. Zahniser and fellow preservationists developed the initial language for a bill submitted to the 84th Congress by Minnesota senator Hubert Humphrey. Its preamble read in part: "to secure for the American people of present and future generations the benefits of an enduring reservoir of wilderness." The bill listed 160 parks, forests, monuments, preserves, and even Indian reservations that might constitute such a system. Between June 1957 and May 1964, Congress devoted more time to wilderness bill hearings than it had on any other conservation measure in the nation's history. Six thousand pages of testimony were transcribed. The bill was rewritten and reintroduced sixty-six times! Congressmen reported huge volumes of mail from their constituents, mostly written by people with little more exposure to a wilderness than the occasional walk in the woods or a camping overnight, yet firm in their support of the legislation.[181]

Prominent philosophers of conservation like Thoreau and Muir were often quoted in session. Aldo Leopold was singled out as initiator of the modern wilderness movement. During a 1961 Senate hearing, Sierra Club spokesman David Brower put forth that "no man who reads Leopold with an open mind will never again, with clear conscience, testify against the wilderness bill."[182]

Resistance came from all the expected camps: the wood-using industries along with oil, grazing, and mining interests. Their concern was the permanence of reserving so much land, 60 million acres according to one version of the bill. Yet there was criticism from unexpected factions—the National Park Service, for example—believing strongly that a wilderness system was unneeded. Existing agencies, they believed, already served the public's need for a wilderness. The USFS persisted with its multiple-use doctrine, successfully removing all but fifty-four nominated areas, leaving nine million of the proposed 60 million acres still eligible. It was the John Muir vs. Gifford Pinchot debate heard all over again.

In its revised form, the bill passed by a 73–12 Senate vote on April 10, 1963, and a 373–1 House vote on July 30, 1964. President Johnson signed the Wilderness Act into law on September 3, 1964, just two months after another historic signing, the Civil Rights Act of 1964. Both achievements represented high points in President Johnson's career.[183]

Preservationists were at first disappointed with the bill they had fought so hard for. Conservation purists such as Howard Zahnister deplored the need for so many compromises. He watched helplessly as the scope of his original drafting of an "ideal bill" dwindled from sixty million acres to nine million. That the president retained power to approve dams and other public works needed for national security risk meant to him threat of another Hetch Hetchy. And he abhorred the fact that prospecting and mining development might endure for another twenty years or at least until all prior claims had run their course. Yet it was a genuine beginning, the government's first statutory commitment to assuring that some fraction of its land would forever remain wild.

Enactment of the Wilderness Act did not answer the important question about the idea of a managed wilderness. Managed by whom and according to what limitations? If a wilderness can be defined by its distance from humankind, how then does a government assign custodians to regulate visitation? Parameters for designating and administering wilderness were left to the regulation writers. Restrictions on roads, buildings, power lines, pipelines, grazing activity, and timber harvest were stipulated in the bill. Fulfillment of prior contracts, that is mining claims, were limited to a defined period. Like most first of its kind statutes, the Wilderness Act of 1964 had to suffer its own growing pains.

Nonetheless, wilderness as a construct of human civilization was entering a new stage of its history; the "wildeor" was to be appreciated instead of feared. Its scarcity gave it far greater value. Lands protected by the new law would expand and eventually embrace 2 percent of the nation's territorial holdings, about the same fraction that is paved. But even with its shortcomings, the Wilderness Act represented the best hope in sight for a determined band of Eastern Sierrans intent upon stopping another Sierra crossing.[184]

STOPPING THE ROAD

As Governor Reagan brought his 1972 Summit Meadow comments to a close, he emphasized the need for a permanent resolution for what seemed a never-ending road issue. He believed it could be achieved by merging two existing wilderness sanctuaries, thus obliterating the corridor for all time. His audience included forest professionals willing to abandon the trans-Sierra notion but not ready to give up on repairs to the existing road. What should have been apparent to all, however, was that the road issue had been effectively removed from local and regional jurisdiction. Henceforth, the Sierra Nevada's destiny would be decided in Washington, not in the Eastern Sierra, not even in Sacramento.

This didn't mean that the governor was vacating the issue. He followed up by writing California's Democratic senator, Alan Cranston, asking him to consider sponsoring a bill to protect a plot of California land that was "so uniquely suited for wilderness designation that its use for another purpose is unthinkable." Highlighting what he imagined the most feared outcome, Reagan continued: "The cost of a trans-Sierra highway would be outlandishly expensive in relationship to possible use factors." This letter was an important first step in a process that would ultimately lead to passage of the California Wilderness Act of 1984, but not without a dozen more years of acrimonious debate. The fact that Reagan chose Cranston over California's Republican senator, Pete Wilson, merely reflected the governor's savvy about setting in motion an environmental initiative... put it in the hands of a Democrat.[185]

MEANWHILE, LOCAL EFFORTS to block the road had not languished during the lead-up to Governor Reagan's backcountry appearance. Throughout the spring of 1972, Genny Smith's letter-writing habit remained a force to be reckoned with. She had written Lou Roeser about her own efforts to elicit interest from Washington, identifying Sierra Club lobbyist Lloyd Tupling as her point man, and offering to raise money to fly him to California so he could learn about the issue. Her concern was that Ike Livermore was distracted by so many other problems. She was not yet aware that the secretary's initiatives were about to pay off.[186]

Judge Ray Sherwin wrote his own plea to the governor and received a prompt reply: "We are presently engaged in extensive efforts to prevent construction." He enclosed copies of the recent exchange with Secretary Volpe, not very reassuring to the judge's eyes either. Genny Smith, when she learned of Reagan's Summit Meadow statement, knew instantly how significant it was. Sending her own letter of thanks, these kind words were returned by the governor: "Sometimes it gets pretty rugged here in Sacramento, as you can well imagine. I am very grateful for your words of encouragement."[187]

The governor covered his political bases by notifying opposing legislators of his decision. Congressman Sisk's reply began formally, "Dear Mr. Governor," but held nothing back. Expressing personal disbelief in the position taken, he accused the governor of denying many thousands of California citizens what was rightfully theirs. He characterized the publicity event as folly and challenged the governor to prove his prediction of a ruined wilderness landscape. Claiming that the established right-of-way was no longer a valid wilderness, he further demeaned the event: "I do not know how far your pony took you... but I am sure you must have noticed a great difference between the character of the corridor itself and

the Minarets." As he had done many times before, he misrepresent-
ed the John Muir Trail's location by claiming it was already crossed
by a drivable road. Genny Smith had tried to disabuse him of the
notion, but he was not listening.[188]

Furious that a project he believed was favorable to the environment could be stopped by executive decree, he deplored the
absence of consultation with Central Valley citizens. Accusing the
governor of a politically calculated decision, he inquired whether
votes gained in the Bay Area would exceed the votes Reagan had
just lost in the Central Valley. Sisk closed with his traditional list
of advantages to such a road: recreation, commerce, and even an
old chestnut, national defense. Once again there was no mention
of prohibitive cost.

In a detailed rebuttal, very likely drafted by Livermore, each
of Sisk's arguments was countered with widely known facts. The
letter corrected once again the congressman's mistaken idea of
where the John Muir Trail was located and refuted the notion that
corridor terrain was any less scenic. Finally, the governor took particular exception to Sisk's claim that by canceling the road he was
catering to a privileged class with leisure time for a wilderness.
Reagan asked Sisk if he really believed the environmental community was any more privileged than the faction promoting the road
for commercial gain?[189]

It was an exchange that amused some, dismayed others,
yet served little purpose. Neither camp was about to budge. Sisk
pledged that he would never abandon his voters; Reagan closed
with these words: "I would like to state emphatically that there is
absolutely no chance that I will reconsider [my decision]. I also
feel that President Nixon will remain firm in his decision." And so
the fight appeared to be over, but only for the time being.

LIKE THE YEARS between 1968 and 1972, very little of road issue
consequence happened between 1973 and 1978. What was clear
from sporadic correspondence was that Mammoth Lakes citizens
were watching closely for any signs of forest roadwork in their vicinity. Meanwhile, the Forest Service maintained its funding search
for limited repairs to a road they still believed hazardous. Equally

alert was the *Fresno Bee*, reporting on November 4, 1975, that for a modest expenditure of fifty-one thousand dollars from USFS, NPS, and Madera County sources, just three miles of road descending from Minaret Summit to Agnew Meadows had been regraded. No provisions were made for paving nor was there any expectation of increased traffic. The repairs were justified as ordinary maintenance that any road would require.[190]

On June 12, 1977, the *Fresno Bee* reported the award of $1.5 million to the USFS for improving forty-three miles of forest highway out of North Fork in Madera County. This too was justified as routine maintenance to a service road in the Sierra National Forest, never acknowledging that the segment had been included in planning for the I-70 extension. Keeping watch on all of these developments were Ike Livermore, Ray Sherwin, and Genny Smith, whose communications with each other raised questions of some "funny business going on."[191]

Voices of enthusiasm for completion of a trans-Sierra highway could still be heard, some of them from unexpected sources. "Nevada Senate Beats Drums for Minaret Road," read the *Fresno Bee* headline on January 7, 1973. Nevada state senator Rick Blakemore of the Ecology and Resources Committee announced that no better site existed for a new highway. After Blakemore's visit to the Madera County Chamber of Commerce, a spokesman for that group declared, "I can assure you that we in the Central Valley would be willing to visit Central Nevada more frequently if we had a road to travel on."[192]

Meanwhile inquires were being made regarding exact location of the current corridor. Somehow the defined geographic limits had either been misplaced or misinterpreted leading to contradictory maps. In a letter to Smith, Livermore referenced the search for accurate boundaries and warned of renewed efforts by Congressman Sisk to secure the corridor one way or another.[193]

What this all meant for the wary and wise was to get busy on legislation that would unite the two adjacent wilderness areas. To the north and tucked between Yosemite National Park and the corridor lay the 109,500-acre Minarets Wilderness Area, formerly the Mount Dana-Minarets Primitive Area. To the south lay the

John Muir Wilderness Area, derived from the Sierra National Forest. Referring to any or all of this in a sound bite or a brochure would have been unwieldy and so a name had to be found for the corridor itself, one that spoke to the future. Former assemblyman and later congressman Jerome Chappie had previously suggested "San Joaquin Roadless Area," which evolved to the more affirmative "San Joaquin Wilderness Area." For advocacy purposes, a San Joaquin Wilderness Association was formed.[194]

Secretary Livermore was critical of the replacement of "Save the John Muir Trail Association" with "San Joaquin Wilderness Association"; he believed in naming causes for a declared rather than imagined objective but not yet designated wilderness area. "It seems to me that in choosing the latter, you are using a more wordy and less appealing name, but are severing the history of the informal committee's work to date, and are not acknowledging in the name that the reason this is the most important wilderness decision in the 'lower 48' is because it is the key to preserving the integrity of the John Muir Trail." On this one point, his colleagues overruled him. Correspondence soon appeared under the name San Joaquin Wilderness Association. Elegant new stationary featured an appropriate letterhead and an advisory board with representation.[195]

The Wilderness Act of 1964 had already established a working definition of wilderness in the United States: "lands that generally possess a primeval character and influence, which have been affected primarily by the forces of nature, and with the imprint of man's work substantially reduced or ideally unnoticed." The act had initially protected nine million acres of primitive land but created a mechanism for making additions to designated areas. Efforts to enlarge the nation's commitment to wilderness were continuous and always controversial. When a 1978 proposal to convert certain existing national park lands to wilderness status, the *Wall Street Journal* branded it the "Park Barrel Bill." Soon after, President Carter signed the "Endangered American Wilderness Act," and 15.7 million acres were added to the total.[196]

The steps for designating new wilderness areas were made deliberately complex. The process was assigned an acronym, RARE, meaning Roadless Area Review and Evaluation. The USFS

established inventories, beginning in 1967 with sixteen areas total-
ing 750,000 acres and continuing in 1977 with sixty-nine areas or
900,000 acres. Although the intent of RARE I and II was to produce a nationwide recommendation, the opening inventory proved
far too controversial for some states to act upon efficiently. And so
each state would make its own decisions about designating eligible land. For California's inventoried roadless areas, decisions were
made in Washington only after local regional battles were fought.
By the time a California's Wilderness Act was ready for signature,
the law's stipulated boundaries encompassed three million acres.[197]

The goal for Eastern Sierrans now functioning as the San
Joaquin Wilderness Area (SJWA) was unchanged—stopping the
road. But their newly adopted motto was "Closing the Gap." Success depended on whether the corridor could be brought within
one of the inventoried roadless areas, making a wilderness designation possible.

While it might seem ridiculous that the corridor was not precisely defined on maps, the modern age of satellites and global po-
sitioning technology was still a decade away. Topographic study of
the Sierra Nevada in that day depended on the generalities of historic surveys. In this particular case, what the USFS thought was
corridor was not entirely free of political bias. Its multiple use doctrine meant that existing claimants for use of land did have some
say, especially the timber industry and the ski areas. Although the
SJWA wanted as much of the corridor declared roadless as possible, timber companies demanded continued access to lands they
had long harvested and ski areas wanted room to expand their existing slopes. Mammoth Mountain Ski Area was no exception.

Ike Livermore and Ray Sherwin deliberately involved themselves with the boundary question, seeking aid from Hal Thomas,
who had successfully lobbied to bring Mineral King, a subalpine
glacial valley, into Sequoia National Park's wilderness zone. All
three puzzled over Forest Service memos that divided the corridor
into "A" and "B" parcels. In time all parties agreed that the gap to
be closed amounted to 159,000 acres.[198]

Meanwhile, Genny Smith involved herself with seeking an
accommodation with the ski industry. An expert skier herself, she

knew the slopes of Mammoth Mountain and paid close attention to MMSA's aspirations for expansion. In her many letters to the Far West Ski Association (FWSA) and the U. S. Ski Association (USSA), her message was the same. With so many square miles of land available for skiing and for wilderness, compromise shouldn't be so difficult. There ought to be room for both new ski areas and new wilderness areas. After all, many of the same people ski the slopes in winter and hike the trails in summer.[199]

Dave McCoy and his staff were forever examining opportunities to expand their allowed area on Mammoth Mountain. In their "Winter Recreation Master Plan Alternatives," three directions for expansion were cited: 1. Back side of the Mountain; 2. Mountain slopes across Sherwin Meadow from Mammoth Lakes Village (a.k.a. Sherwin Bowl); and 3. San Joaquin Ridge extending north toward June Lake and permitting merger with a smaller ski area there. McCoy, who was initially unwilling to relinquish any of these options, did prepare to lobby congressman Norman Shumway in Washington, if necessary.[200]

Genny Smith and her SJWA colleagues sought release only of the back side of Mammoth Mountain, which directly faced the corridor. She knew what McCoy and his operations staff knew as well: most of the existing ski slopes were on the north and eastern faces; the back side faced south and west, where both quantity and quality of snow diminished faster, leaving an unreliable base long before the ski season ended. Smith thought she had received a verbal agreement from Dave McCoy not to contest the most recent corridor boundary, which included much of the back side. But to her chagrin, his willingness to lobby Congress indicated a change of heart. When challenged, McCoy said he was a man of his word. To Smith's delight, Dave's son Gary McCoy replied to a Bureau of Public Roads inquiry, making clear that MMSA would not object to wilderness designation for the southwest face of Mammoth Mountain as long as the privilege of accessing San Joaquin Ridge remained unchanged.[201]

An important exchange of letters between the SJWA and Democratic congressman Philip Burton commenced in 1978 when the legislator demonstrated enthusiasm for sponsoring a California wilderness initiative. Burton, a World War II veteran, practicing attorney, former mayor of San Francisco, and California assembly-man, had served as a representative for eleven terms and earned heroic stature from Eastern Sierrans because of his persistent re-submission of revised wilderness bills.[202]

As momentum for the initiative grew, there were letters to write, fact sheets to print, and newsletters to distribute. Smith al-ways contributed more than her share to the effort. She worried about the terms her colleagues used and was a stickler for geo-graphic accuracy. In one memo she called attention to chronic overuse of a word: "I rarely read a proposal for protection of land that doesn't use the word 'unique,' sometimes appropriately but more often improperly. Features of the Middle Fork Canyon make it beautiful but not unique. Also, the metamorphic rock of the Rit-ter Range is part of a belt that extends all the way from McGee Creek to Tioga Canyon, hardly unique."

The same went for most of the trees—red fir, lodge pole pine, and hemlock were all ecologically typical, she reminded. The Jeffrey Pine forest east of San Joaquin Ridge, however, *was* unique, as were the minaret spires of the Ritter Range. And watch out for calling all rock formation granite ridges; the North Fork and Mid-dle Fork Canyons aren't granite, she reported. As author of the re-gion's best guidebook, her authority was established. Furthermore, she had listened to so much misinformation from the opposing forces that she insisted that "close the gap" testimony be accurate to the word.[203]

Congressman Burton's travail intensified in 1981 with two parallel bills that were introduced: H.R. 856, designating 1.4 mil-lion acres of national park land; and H.R. 859, designating another 2.1 million acres of national forestland. Transitioning NPS territo-ry to wilderness status was less difficult. Converting forestland was the greater challenge. Burton was considered a deft manager of bills in play on the house floor and rose to the occasion.[204]

Ike Livermore, Ray Sherwin, and Genny Smith all appeared before the house committee in support of H.R. 859, supporting in-clusion of the San Joaquin Roadless Area. Making clear that she had come at her own expense, Smith established her authority: "I am not here to drop names," she began, "but I want you to know that all three of us are third- or fourth-generation Californians; we have worked together for twenty years to achieve wilderness status for the San Joaquin. We have collectively devoted 115 summers in the area and nearly as many winters; we are responsible citizens who work for a living. We understand that the boundary proposals will not give the wilderness people, or the skiers, or the timber interests 100 percent of what they want, but this compromise is a balanced proposal fair to all."[205]

Next she turned to the poster, carried over from her Sacramento testimony against A.B. 290. Her goal was to acquaint everyone attending the hearing with the odds against keeping any major highway through the corridor open and useful throughout the year. For reference, there was Donner Summit at 7,200 feet, a highway that ascended gradually, passed through a short segment above the 6,000-foot snow line, then descended at the same steady rate. But a highway through the corridor would have to rise to 7,000 feet, descend to 5,000 feet, climb to 9,000 feet, return to 7,000 feet, climb again to 9,000 feet, before arriving in Mammoth Lakes at 8,000 feet. It was terrain that one highway engineer insisted would require one or more tunnels, exceptional tunnels many times longer than the lone 1.6-mile tunnel beneath Colorado's Independence Pass.

The zone familiar to some as "the corridor" and to others as "the gap" was assuming the shape of an amoeba, its many pseudopods pointing in all directions at once. One of these projected southward to encompass Lake Edison. A second smaller one extended northward from Minaret Summit to Agnew Meadow, while a third embraced the back side of Mammoth Mountain. Most important was the largest pseudopod directed westward past Summit Meadow and Iron Mountain toward North Fork, removing any doubt about what the battle was all about.[206]

Convincing testimony notwithstanding, there were additional hurdles to clear and many more votes to come. Burton's two bills were eventually combined into H.R. 4083, which on July 17, 1981, passed the House on a voice vote. Unfortunately, its US Senate version, introduced by Sen. Alan Cranston, did not achieve the same success. This meant starting all over again, with resubmission of the bill in the 98th Congress as H.R. 1437. Regrettably, Burton would not live to see his bill pass on April 12, 1983, by a vote of 297–96. His colleagues later mused that "had Phil known he might not live, he would have put a lot more wilderness into his bill."[207]

The task now fell upon Alan Cranston to carry forward into Senate proceedings the late congressman's aspirations for wilderness expansion. He enlisted the aid of fellow senator Pete Wilson, a Republican, who as an assemblyman had served on the Transportation and Commerce Committee that rejected both A.B. 290 and A.B. 1191, keeping FH100 out of the state highway system. Between them they would bring into balance both the unrealistic demands of environmentalists and the impractical claims of myriad commercial interests. Both Cranston and Wilson wanted a successful bill.[208]

Meanwhile, Fresno and Madera Counties rallied their forces when the rapid advance of legislation likely to eradicate the corridor and its highway potential became clear. Because so much time had elapsed since prior road debates, *Fresno Bee* reporters had to redefine the issue for their readers. Editors could not recall whether to refer to the Mammoth Pass Road or the Minaret Summit Highway. Chamber of Commerce members broke out the old justifications—including iron ore mining, year-round recreation access, and once again national defense—all of this while omitting mention of past highway department misgivings. When it was learned that the Federal Highway Administration had appropriated $2 million for construction of an escape route from Mammoth Lakes to CA 395 in case of earthquake, Maderans wanted to know why they couldn't have their own mountain escape route?[209]

While the Senate continued its deliberation of the Burton bill, Senator Cranston's office was asked repeatedly to answer concerns about rumored boundary revisions. In fact, the original 159,000-acre corridor had been reduced to 110, 000 acres, compromises having been made to hydroelectric interests, cattle grazers, and the timber industry. This was far better than the USFS recommendation to limit wilderness designation to 47,000 acres. At 110,000 acres and without further revisions, H.R. 1437 would permanently eliminate for all time the corridor's right-of-way.[210]

Still recognized on the senate floor as "Phil Burton's Bill," it passed easily on September 28, 1983, but legislative procedure required a conference committee to bring the final products of both houses into accommodation. Another year of horse trading was required to yield a bill eligible for signature. The California Wilderness Act of 1983 would thus become the Omnibus California Wilderness Act of 1984. Land parcels in national parks were never in contention, whereas lands in national forests were deliberated to the end. Meanwhile, Madera County supervisor George Kennedy called for a "last ditch campaign to save the corridor... even if it takes 20–30 years to build a road." But Senator Cranston's office made clear that it was too late for last-ditch efforts. The senator had in fact secured nine thousand more acres of corridor for the wilderness.[211]

The fate of the corridor may be unique in legislative annals. A previously designated Minarets Wilderness doubled in size from 110,000 to 229,000 acres. Its name vanished because of a newly defined wilderness named for Ansel Adams. The news came as a shock to Eastern Sierrans; what had Adams done to aid their cause. Hadn't he pleaded for the road to be built?[212]

The giant amoeba was by now even larger, sending another long pseudopod northward toward Yosemite National Park, encompassing Mount Dana but stopping short of the Tioga Road, its entire shape recognizable to any politician whose election district had been "gerrymandered".[213]

Without celebration or a press statement, on September 28, 1984 President Reagan signed Public Law 98-425, as the California Wilderness Act would be recorded in the nation's statute book. His administration had fought to limit the Burton Bill because of its perceived overly broad sweep. The president's position didn't surprise supporters of the legislation; Reagan's environmental record as a governor was by then largely forgotten. While it is interesting to suppose that he knew that Section 101, Articles 15 and 25 canceled forever the highway he once fought himself, there is no record of him tracking the bill's progress or showing special interest in the corridor's fate.[214]

One year later, Genny Smith and Ike Livermore exchanged letters reflecting on their victory. He recalled a half-century and she a quarter-century of struggle to stop a road for all time. She apologized for "not having the oomph" to write or phone anyone after the bill was signed. All she remembered was a feeling of relief. Although she had once imagined a big event to celebrate the San Joaquin Wilderness, it didn't happen. Maybe the unexpected name change had dispatched the idea.[215]

Nobody understands for certain how the new wilderness was named for the Sierra Nevada's iconic photographer Ansel Adams. Did he have influential friends in high places? Wilderness Society executive director William Turnage, was his good friend and presumably his successful advocate. Adams had initially offered his name to the cause, but he later accused the region around Minaret Summit to be uninteresting at best, one of the ironies of this road story. Nonetheless, his name currently adorns all trail entries into the Ansel Adams Wilderness Area.[216]

Proud conservation organizations issued bulletins citing the enormous environmental achievements of 1984. William Turnage considered the final outcome historic in scope: 8.6 million acres designated as wilderness throughout twenty-one states, more than during any prior year since 1964, when the Wilderness Act became law. The California bill was the most controversial of any of the state initiatives but also the largest in terms of acreage added to the system: 1.4 million acres of national parkland and 1.8 million acres of national forestland. In addition, the bill assigned National Scenic Area status to 66,000 acres surrounding Mono Lake in the Eastern Sierra. Eighty-three miles of the Tuolumne River became part of the Wild and Scenic Rivers System. Also remarkable, but less well publicized, was the precedent-setting release of 2.4 million acres from any further wilderness consideration. It was one of the features that justified Genny Smith's testimonial on behalf of a balanced bill deserving affirmation.[217]

The original corridor and its supplemental appendages now represent 4 percent of the total land redesignated by California's

Bob and Peggy Schotz also pleased… they stopped the road!
CREDIT: *Bob Schotz*

biggest wilderness initiative to date. Yet the single-minded determination of relatively few people made a very great difference in
the legislation's outcome. Ike Livermore said it best when, long before victory, he observed that closing the corridor would not only
"settle a dispute that has been going on for fifty years," but also, "in-
sure the integrity of the world famous 211-mile John Muir Trail,
which is the longest stretch of trail unbroken by roads in the lower 48 states." A hard-fought battle for change involving only 5 percent of lands governed by U. S. Public Law 98-425 did just that.[218]

Genny flashes her smile that must have greeted news of the California Wilderness Act becoming law.
CREDIT: *Genny Smith*

"WE WERE LUCKY"

WHENEVER GENNY SMITH recalls twenty-seven years of personal involvement in her "campaign against the road," she likes to attribute success to "a few lucky breaks." Whenever she speaks to organizations about the experience, she lists some of the unexpected happenings that contributed to victory—for example, a postponed hearing that allowed more time to prepare, or else find a new ally. But luck wasn't everything unless one believes like Machiavelli that human events are largely determined by *fortuna*. Luck aside, what influences success are vigilance, curiosity, skepticism, focus, verification, challenge, and determination. Genny Smith practiced them all. These behaviors aside, here are some events she listed as her own "fortuna."[219]

FIRST LUCKY BREAK:
"Hearing delayed."

"A.B. 290 WAS scheduled for committee discussion on April 4, 1967. So many road opponents showed up that, for reasons never explained (I have long wondered if it was our numbers), the hearing was postponed for two weeks. Nonetheless, I believe the delay might have been the luckiest break of all because it afforded me the opportunity to meet and later coordinate with Ike Livermore, the 'most important asset the campaign could possibly have."

SECOND LUCKY BREAK:
"My first encounter with Ike Livermore."

"A SIERRA CLUB Wilderness Conference just one week after the postponement allowed me opportunity to hear luncheon speaker Livermore assail advocates for another trans-Sierra highway. That was a clear turning point for us; here was a respected Republican, old family, member of Reagan's cabinet, and passionate about no new roads in the Sierra. Up to this point we were a handful of ordinary people with no connections; now we had an important political ally."

THIRD LUCKY BREAK:
"Newspaper headlines throughout the state."

"THE CONFERENCE WAS attended by a *San Francisco Chronicle* reporter whom I realized was unaccustomed to covering environmental issues and knew nothing about the Minaret Summit Road issue. So I made certain that he spoke to people who could fill him in with the facts. Next morning, my efforts resulted in a *San Francisco Chronicle* feature article under a large anti-road headline and an accompanying editorial to boot. What's more, the story was picked up in newspapers throughout California. So our issue had hit the big time . . . we thought maybe we might succeed!"

FOURTH LUCKY BREAK:
"A professional who cared about the Sierra."

"ONLY A FEW days remained until the rescheduled A.B. 290 hearing and I had no idea where to begin with publicity. So I contacted the person who masterminded the publicity for the recent Wilderness Conference and received advice about which news desks to contact, which editorial writers were most friendly to the issue. Never before had I even thought I could produce so much news favorable to our cause."

FIFTH LUCKY BREAK:
"A conversation in the Ladies Room."

THE WILDERNESS CONFERENCE was attended by UC–Davis students representing a campus organization, Active Conservation Tactics (ACT). "During a break, we talked about the road issue; I asked one of the students if she would like to attend a hearing and her eyes lit up." ACT students attended in force. A spokesman, Robert Schneider, distinguished himself as one of the stars." Meanwhile, Transportation Committee members learned that college students actually cared enough to attend and participate.[220]

SIXTH LUCKY BREAK:
"Timely letter from a trucker."

"WE WERE HAVING a hard time with Fresno arguments that a road was absolutely essential for a needed major east-west truck route. Was it? We didn't know. Sierra Club member Francis Wolcott suggested we contact someone he knew in the trucking industry. We did. After we explained the issue to an officer of Pacific Intermountain Express, he obliged with a strong opinion on appropriate stationery. The proposed route would be far too steep a grade to serve as an economic truck route. Important lesson learned… always go to the primary source for accurate information. We road warriors knew we had to go into hearings armed with more facts than our opponents were even aware of."

SEVENTH LUCKY BREAK:
"When we needed posters for hearings…"

"ONE OF OUR supporters was an architect. When we needed to emphasize our point about road costs, she made some eye-catching posters and for free! My favorite was the graphic showing how the proposed road was so much higher than I-80 over Donner Summit. That one sat on an easel where committee members could not help looking at it for the entire day. And it was available years later for hearings in Washington, DC."

EIGHTH LUCKY BREAK:
"An old political hand."

"WE WERE ALL such novices." Later in the campaign, the boyfriend of a supporter offered his help. A city official who had learned the ropes after many years of experience, he advised Genny and her colleagues on who to see and what to say and when.

GENNY SMITH OFTEN spoke of the satisfaction she derived from reminding congressmen that some of the important players who helped fight the road at the state level had moved on to federal responsibilities. She came to Washington prepared to pull from her file correspondence from former assemblyman Pete Wilson turned US senator, former California budget director Casper Weinberger turned White House budget director, and best of all former governor Ronald Reagan turned president of the United States.[221]

Her list of providential events might have been longer had she polled her colleagues. There were many more champions and plenty of reasons for success. First and foremost was Ike Livermore's early commitment to maintaining a roadless Sierra wilderness. As a young man embarking on his first Sierra adventures, he had recognized the incongruity of pickup trucks so close to an iconic trail. Just as important as his ensuing climb to a position of power was his capacity to organize actionable plans. Without the political synchrony of a Livermore and a Reagan, early progress toward victory might never have occurred; without the timely concurrence of Nixon and his largely Californian staff, important steps to success might never have occurred.

Judge Ray Sherwin was the appropriate partner for Ike Livermore in terms of family heritage and comprehensive familiarity with the terrain. Political savvy notwithstanding, the judge's ability to monitor and maneuver within the legislative process provided advantage for the road opponents that road advocates could never match.

Citizens of Fresno and Madera Counties had their own lineup of champions. Assemblymen Mobley and Zenovich, along with Congressman Sisk, stood out because of their untiring perseverance. They were all familiar with the sentiments and desires of their constituents, and they did what democratically elected representatives are supposed to do: fight for appropriations and statutes that best serve local interests. Their only failing was to consistently ignore facts that invalidated their position.

Central to arguments against the road was lack of any business or economic justification. Genny Smith put it like this: "I was only a tree hugger; politicians never listen to people like me. But they'll listen to businessmen, and we had good ones who made their case at hearing after hearing." Notions of untapped mineral wealth were never confirmed; state mining surveys revealed no more than trifling deposits. Not even the USFS believed that more roads meant improved timber yields; millions might be spent for only a few thousand dollars gain. Tourism as a motive didn't count for much if the road was only accessible during summer months. A typical winter snowpack melts very slowly at 9,000 feet.

Specious arguments like national defense or nuclear threat hardly justified the time required for investigation but road opponents did their homework anyway. Military authorities made clear that the movement of ordnance from inland depots to coastal installations depended on railroads, not highways, and certainly not an undependable mountain road. As for escape from nuclear attack, a narrow winding thoroughfare was worthless for evacuating millions from the Central Valley. Yet these implausible motives were voiced time and again.

Government agencies closely involved with the disputed corridor were committed to longstanding policies—for example, guaranteeing multiple usage of the national forests and seasonal access to the national parks. Neither agency was willing to relinquish land already within their jurisdiction; both relished the additions to current holdings. Policies were sometimes modified when leadership changed. In the final analysis, both agencies were willing to give up the notion of a thoroughfare, but neither budged on maintaining existing road safety.

Only one government bureau stood by its original conclusion: the California Division of Highways. Undeterred by the dithering of its federal counterpart, the US Bureau of Public Roads, California's highway engineers conducted their own studies and arrived at what initially seemed contradictory positions; namely, it was possible to build a highway of any dimension through the corridor, but to build such a road was folly. Knowing that infrastructure budgets were always limited, they insisted time and again that state funds not be used for any phase of development of the Minaret Summit highway project. In this case state opinion prevailed over the federal position because it would be the responsibility of California authorities to maintain the road. Throughout the controversy, the highway report was always the deal breaker but only if all parties were listening, and they weren't.

Environmental advocacy groups assumed the posture expected of them: they were against all roads. Only the Sierra Club was forced to reverse an earlier decision and join late in resisting all new trans-Sierra roads. Sport fishermen wrote letters urging their elected representatives to keep the wilderness remote for wild fishing, while deer hunters wanted a sparsely traveled backcountry free of lunatics shooting out of the backs of their Jeeps.

Despite an impressive lineup of proponents and opponents, there was still a political process to be followed. While Ike Livermore could recall fifty years of involvement with the issue and Genny Smith twenty-seven, Judge Sherwin's engagement was somewhere between. The actual legislative process endured for twenty-three years, from introduction of Senate Joint Resolution 43 to bring the "Mammoth Pass Road" into the Forest Highway System (1961) until the California Wilderness Act became law (1984). Dealing with the road question in Sacramento consumed two independent legislative cycles over the span of seven years, resulting in consistent denial of state funding. Deliberations over federal funding options lasted another four years until an unprecedented presidential decree put another stop to the process. Another twelve years were required to convert the corridor into a protected wilderness.

Whether or not one believes this was too long to resolve what some considered a petty issue has to be judged in the context of other historic impasses like temperance, civil rights, and abortion. Political historians familiar with democracy in America would not consider a twenty-three-year conflict unusual for resolving any contentious issue.[222]

The irony of an environmental victory being achieved largely by Republicans instead of by Democrats should not be overlooked. Yet the road controversy was never a partisan issue. One of the sponsors of road legislation was Republican, the other Democrat. Eastern Sierra opponents of the road were more liberal than conservative in their electoral habits, but they were fighting to sustain an existing business model as much as they were fighting for a natural sanctuary. The fact that Livermore, Reagan, Weinberger, and Nixon were all Republicans had less to do with the outcome than that they were all Californians who understood and surely benefited from their state's spectacular geography.

Genny Smith summed it up this way: "With all those people against us how did we win? We were ordinary people without money and without connections! But if you are willing to hang in longer than your opposition and the facts are on your side, then you may surprise yourself and win."

EPILOGUE

O N FRIDAY AFTERNOON of a President's Day weekend, snow has been falling in the Sierra Nevada continuously for the past two days. Because of a massive cold front coming off the Pacific Ocean, the forecast is for a week of snow and sleet. Meanwhile, a bright sun commands the sky in the San Joaquin Valley where dense holiday traffic bound for the ski slopes or Lake Tahoe's gambling casinos is already heading east out of the Greater Sacramento Area via Interstate 80.

Already on full alert are the California Department of Transportation (Caltrans) and the California Highway Patrol (CHP). Storms of this intensity are expected to impede mountain traffic a dozen times each winter season. Meticulous coordination involving both agencies is therefore required. On this particular weekend, 250 Caltrans District 3 personnel committed to their respective tasks are distributed among command centers extending from Auburn to Stateline, a 76-mile highway segment that rises from 1,400 to 7,239 feet at Donner Summit. Average daily traffic over this mountain pass can reach 40,000 vehicles. But on a holiday weekend, the number may rise to 50,000, including 6,000 heavy trucks. Add heavy snowfall to the equation and road capacity falls to 1,000 vehicles per hour, less than half of the normal flow.[223]

In order to avoid closure of one of the busiest commercial thoroughfares in the nation, Caltrans will operate 150 specially equipped vehicles around the clock: plows, sanders, deicers, graders, loaders, fuel trucks, and the heaviest duty tow trucks. Assisting the trucking industry during storms on I-80 are the "pusher trucks" owned and maintained by the California Trucking Association but operated by Caltrans, a joint venture supporting transport of goods over Donner Summit. These enormous vehicles are capable of extricating eighteen-wheelers from obstructive predicaments that could snarl traffic for hours before this program. I-80 is almost never closed for snow accumulation alone; rare closures are imposed for limited visibility or else vehicle obstruction.

Winter weekend operations for Caltrans and the CHP take into account that sport enthusiasts will have anticipated weather conditions by dressing themselves appropriately and remembering to pack their tire chains. But 70 percent of motorists encountered on I-80 lack experience driving in snow conditions. Caltrans and CHP personnel on scene make decisions about chain control based on the least capable driver. Given deteriorating road conditions, one in four vehicles will be turned back for lack of chains.

On this particular weekend, motorists begin their climb from the Central Valley floor while flashing signs announce that traffic will be metered (reduced) beyond the Applegate exit. What this means is that access to higher elevations is limited to a predetermined number of vehicles passing each hour. In practice, three lanes of traffic are narrowed to two, and several miles later, two lanes are reduced to one.

Caltrans and the CHP understand that cars and trucks do not mix well on road surfaces encrusted with snow and ice. I-80 being one of the busiest commercial thoroughfares in the nation, truckers are assigned priority on weekdays. But on weekends, private motorists are given priority eastbound on Friday, westbound on Sunday. On this Friday afternoon, hundreds of eighteen-wheelers are already diverted from the highway and parked on frontage roads bordering I-80. They await clearance that will come late in the evening and continue throughout the night when truckers again dominate the highway.[224]

Another hour will pass before passenger traffic is metered to a single lane of vehicles moving forward at low speed. Suddenly, the shoulder widens as a "chain-on area" is reached. Always placed near an exit, these are zones where the ill-equipped motorist is identified and turned back. For all others, ample space is provided to personally apply chains or else commission experts to attach chains for a specified fee. Only for motorists in a hurry does metering represent an intolerable frustration. Sensible holiday travelers are grateful for regulated traffic policies that usually get them to their destination safely although not necessarily on time.

The costs for this regulation of traffic are not insignificant. Caltrans spends $10 million annually for snow removal at Donner Summit, nearly 20 percent of the State of California's entire snow clearance budget! Fortunately, costs per vehicle are coming down because of more advanced equipment and better coordination of the combined agency effort.

At the southern end of Lake Tahoe, another year-round trans-Sierra route, US 50, crosses Echo Summit at 7,381 feet. Not an interstate, it draws fewer commercial vehicles than I-80 but nearly as many recreational motorists, thereby requiring full agency coordination and another major budget appropriation.

IN STARK CONTRAST, four to seven months will pass with almost no human presence in a wilderness zone that lies between North Fork in the Sierra Nevada foothills and Minaret Summit in the Eastern Sierra, a realized dream first envisioned by people determined to rescue the Sierra Nevada from road builders. A peaceful sanctity exists on this President's Day weekend as storm clouds form and gradually engulf surrounding peaks. Both flora and fauna are adapted to seasonal cold fronts and the precipitation they bring.

Because of continuous snowfall, US 41 rising out of Fresno toward Yosemite National Park is already restricted to vehicles with chains. The USFS Scenic Byway out of North Fork, formerly designated as FH 100, is closed to all traffic for the season. Practical wilderness access is limited to the occasional snowmobiler or cross-country skier. Only a rare winter trekker will venture beyond Clover Meadow. In the Eastern Sierra, CA 203 beyond the Mammoth Mountain Ski Area's Main Lodge has been closed since November. Ski patrollers monitor the area's boundaries and restrict skiers from access to the back-side slopes leading down to Reds Meadow and the surrounding valley floor.

For the rare mid-winter visitor, the Sierra Nevada dressed in its wintry attire is a place distinct from its summertime counterpart, first documented by Orland Bartholomew whose 1928–29 diary records the first winter ascent of Mount Whitney and subsequent three-hundred-mile Sierra trek. Far from being a silent refuge, it can be a raucous zone where thunderclaps of distant avalanches are heard regularly throughout the winter season. No less conspicuous is the periodic moaning of gale-force winds sending giant plumes of snow off distant peaks. Diminishing temperatures set the dry tree bark to crackling while the distant howling of coyotes interrupts the stillness.[225]

Winter wildlife viewing might include the bounding Sierra hares, foraging mice, and the occasional solitary porcupine, none of which share with the North American black bear a seasonal requirement for hibernation. A bounty of chickadees and nuthatches remain in residence year-round because of their intrinsic cold tolerance. No longer represented are regionally extinct wolverines and wolves, which were still present for Mr. Bartholomew's viewing in the late 1920s.

All the while there is plenty of snow in varied formats, light and powdery, granular and abrasive, wind-packed and ice-crusted. The best snow for conveyance of man or beast lies between 7,000 and 10,000 feet. Depth varies according to season, altitude, and bearing. As ground cover, it can be spare in late autumn but copious by President's Day weekend, rarely more than one or two feet on wind exposed surfaces but often greater than ten feet in protected hollows, canyons, and chutes. As the ambient temperature begins to rise, frequent reminders of unexpected snow and ice movement interrupt the peace ... perhaps a thunderous roar of tumbling snow or else a piercing crack of slab ice breaking free of sheer canyon walls.

Together with the onset of spring come signs of animal activity. Where hidden pools of water are revealed beneath melting shelves of ice, a chorus of croaking frogs might be heard. Beavers reappear, having subsisted on stored food in lodges integral to self-made dams. Hibernating ground squirrels reawaken to six months of warm season activity, and mule deer return from their winter ranges at lower altitude. An indolent stream suddenly becomes a torrent overflowing trails worn by summertime hikers. As snowdrifts gradually recede and ground water subsides, humankind will return to those revealed trails, some riding saddle stock, many more on foot as hikers or campers.

All of this and more, 200-plus miles more of protected wilderness terrain uninterrupted by vehicle transit, all because of a few people who cared so much they persevered for decades to stop a road.

Sierra solitude… undisturbed
CREDIT: *Stephen Ingram*

APPENDIX I

CHRONOLOGY IN SUPPORT OF *Stopping the Road*

Key to Sources:

AAL	Ansel Adams letters
AR	Adele Reed, *Old Mammoth*
BL	Bancroft Library
BSP	Bob and Peggy Schotz papers
BTP	Bob Tanner papers
CSL	California State Library
CTL	Caltrans Library
CVI	Chip Van Nattan interview
DBL	David Brower letter April 1956
DFL	Dorothy Fitzhugh letter
DPW	Department of Public Works (Samuel B. Nelson report)
DDI	Deanna Dulen interview
DMI	Dave McCoy interview
EC	Ella Cain, *Story of Mono County*
FBL	*Fresno Bee* Library
FF	Francis Farquhar, *History of the Sierra Nevada*
GSP	Genny Smith papers, personal and in Bancroft Library
LRP	Lou and Marye Roesser papers
NLP	Norman Livermore papers
RM	Robin Morning, *Tracks of Passion*
RNL	Richard Nixon Presidential Library
RRL	Ronald Reagan Presidential Library
SCB	*Sierra Club Bulletin*
SFC	*San Francisco Chronicle*
WP	*Washington Post*

Chronology

1542: Juan Rodriguez Cabrillo assigns name "Sierras Nevadas" to Coastal Range within sight. Name sticks, but for more easterly range. (FF)

1772: Pedro Fages, traveling east, ascends Cajon Pass, then crosses a vast desert beyond, observes a great range to the north. (FF)

1826: Jedediah Smith party crosses Sierra Nevada near Ebbetts Pass. [FF]

1833: Joseph Walker party crosses Sierra Nevada, finds Yosemite Valley.(FF)

1841: John Bidwell party crosses Sierra Nevada near Sonora Pass. [FF]

1843: Lt. John Fremont party crosses Sierra Nevada near Carson Pass, finds Lake Tahoe. [FF]

1846: Donner Party trapped in early snow during Truckee River ascent. [FF]

1849: Gold discovered by John Sutter; California becomes a magnet for thousands willing to endure hardship for pursuit of gold. [FF]

1855: California passes first "Act to Construct a Wagon Road over the Sierra Nevada." [FF]

1856: First publicly funded wagon road over Sierra Nevada is built from Murphy, CA, to Carson Valley, according to Ella Cain. [EC]

1864: State of California appropriates $400,000 to build a road from Sonora in Tuolomne County to Bridgeport in Mono County. [EC]

1869: Central Pacific and Union Pacific tracks joined in Promontory, Utah.

1870: James L. C. Sherwin begins Sherwin Toll Road out of Bishop, CA. [AR]

1877: Gen. George Dodge commits funds to "Mineral Hill" near Pumice Mountain, later named Mammoth Mountain after short-lived Mammoth City. [AR]

1901: Southern Pacific Railroad survey for road over Mammoth Pass cited in CA 203 file. [CTL]

1910: Inyo Good Road Club launched; governor visits Eastern Sierra. [RM]

1911: President Taft designates Devils Postpile a national monument. [DDI]

1912: AAA installs eight hundred road signs between Los Angeles and Lake Tahoe on a road called El Camino Sierra, later named Three flags Highway and then CA 23 [RM]

1915: Great Sierra Wagon Road joins private road built from Lee Vining over Tioga Pass. [RM]

1916: Opening of improved highway from Bishop to "upper country." Travel time to Mammoth Lakes reduced to two and a half hours. It is still referred to as Sherwin Grade. Instructions: Always fill radiator at Paradise Camp. [RM]

1920: Lake Mary Road built by US Forest Service (USFS) for four thousand dollars plus private gifts. [AR]

1925: California Division of Highways improves CA 23 from Mojave to Bishop. [RM]

1928: Edna McCoy and her son, Dave, arrive in Eastern Sierra. [RM]

1929: Mining company completes construction of first vehicular road from Mammoth Lakes to the Minarets Creek outlet. [CTL]

1930: USFS "Primitive Areas" established (with preservation of a corridor to permit later development of another trans-Sierra road). [GSP]

1931: High Sierra and Minarets Primitive Areas designated by Department of Agriculture; the corridor lying between them is preserved for multiple use. [DPW]

1931: Mammoth residents first express opposition to another trans-Sierra highway. [CTL]

1933: S.B. 563 first proposes including a Mammoth Pass highway into the California highway system (maintenance only, no construction). [CTL]

1935: El Camino Sierra (a.k.a. CA 23) becomes US 395 [RM]

1937: New road exiting CA 395 designated State Route 112 (later CA 203) also becomes Mammoth Lake's Main Street. [CTL]

1938: Dave McCoy first skis Mammoth Mountain with Rey family. [RM]

1938: Ike Livermore writes an essay, "Roads Running Wild," for *American Forests.* [NLP]

1938: Conservation leaders meet with USFS to voice opposition to all proposed trans-Sierra routes south of Tioga Pass. [CTL]

1939: February 19, Fresno Bee story, "Maderans Back North Fork to Nevada Route," states road is for defense purposes; cites Army[sic] and Hawthorne. [FBL]

1946: USFS survey assigns low ranking to Mammoth Mountain. for recreational ski area development. [RM]

1946: State Division of Mines study shows that ore content of samples from Iron Mountain is poor. [GSP]

1946; On June 18, Fresno and Madera County Chambers of Commerce (FCCC, MCCC) join forces in support of "Mammoth Pass Road" providing access to timber, magnesium, iron, lead, silver, tungsten, and recreation. [FBL]

1947: Sierra Club changes position, opposes all trans-Sierra roads. [DBL].

1948: USFS begins construction of timber access road through Chiquita Basin to Graveyard Meadows. [CTL]

1949: Mono County improves Minaret Road to Mammoth Mountain Ski Area (MMSA) (24-foot road bed with 8 percent maximum grade, 250-foot minimum radius). [CTL]

1953: August 15 *Fresno Bee* story says Madera County supervisor visits Chiquita Basin, agrees on need for Mammoth Pass Road to Reds Meadow and Agnew Pass [sic]. [FBL]

1953: Minaret Road paved to MMSA and Minaret Summit beyond. [RM]

1954: August 25 *Fresno Bee* editorial published: "Must have way to get out in case of enemy bombing attack." [FBN]

1955: CA Assembly Joint Resolution 5 and Senate Joint Resolution 43 petitions Congress to finance a trans-Sierra highway at Mammoth Pass. [GSP]

1955: CA Assembly Joint Resolution 8 petitions Congress to have Mammoth Pass Road constructed as a National Defense Highway. [DPW].

1956: President Eisenhower signs into law the Federal-Aid Highway Act 1956 (a.k.a. Interstate Highway and Defense Act 1956). [WP]

1956: Inyo County supervisor endorses trans-Sierra highway at Mammoth Pass. [CTL]

1956: Mono County supervisor conditionally endorses a trans-Sierra highway [CTL].

1956: USFS, Bureau of Public Roads (BPR), and California Division of Highways join in seeking feasibility study of proposed Mammoth Pass Road. [CTL].

1956: BPR survey: "no question of desirability of a shorter route from Central Valley to points east"; USFS cites limited forest highway budget, says Highway and Defense Act definitely offers better source. [DPW].

1957: *Sierra Club Bulletin* states opposition to trans-Sierra highway at Porterville or at Mammoth Pass. [CTL]

1957: Feasibility study finds route practicable from engineering and construction standpoint. Three agencies agree to further study regarding traffic potential and economic feasibility. [CTL]

1957: First petition circulated and signed by numerous citizens of Mammoth Lakes. [Dfl]

1957: BPR revises earlier report to feasible only if aligned with Minaret Summit. [DPW] [CTL]

1957: On July 23, Ansel Adams joins fight against Mammoth Pass Road. [AAL]

1958: Additional resurfacing 4.1 miles of Minaret Road between CA 203 and Mammoth Mountain Ski Area. CA 203 previously extended to Horseshoe. [CTL].

1958: In the November 18, *Fresno Bee* story, "MPR Backed by U.S. Agency," the U.S. Bureau of Public Roads declares Mammoth Pass crossing feasible and important. [FBL] [CTL]

1958: Genny Smith writes "Dear People" memo, soliciting letters be written in response to news of field study results by Sheridan Farin. [GSP]

1958: Dorothy Fitzhugh helps Genny Smith write and distribute ninety petitions against road (she received 1,304 signatures). [Dfl]

1959: In a May 22 *Fresno Bee* story, Fresno attorney Chester Warlow cites National Park Service (NPS) support of Mammoth Pass Road (but NPS makes clear it doesn't want to tell the USFS what to do). [FBL].

1959: An August 8 story in the *Fresno Bee* reports about the Sierra Nevada trek of William O. Douglas, associate justice of the U.S. Supreme Court, and states that Douglas opposes the Mammoth Pass Road. [FBL].

1959: Mono County superviser opposes routing of Mammoth Pass Road recommended by the Bureau of Public Roads and says it is not feasible for all-year highway. [FBL] [CTL]

1960: In a January 8 *Fresno Bee* story, Sterling Cramer of Yosemite Park Curry Company proposes Minarets Wilderness be added to Yosemite and that the NPS be responsible for the Mammoth Pass Road. [FBL].

1961: Notice of public hearing on Mammoth Pass Road by the Bureau of Public Roads given. [GSP]

1961: Lou Roeser letter cites the high cost of Tioga Road despite winter closure. [GSP]

1961: On May 16, a hearing in Fresno reported that strong opposition voiced by Sierra Club, Wilderness Society, Nature Conservancy; citizen demands her right to fresh lettuce (from Nevada?). [FBL]

1961: California Senate Joint Resolution 43 to include Mammoth Pass Road in USFS highway system is approved. [DPW].

1962: USFS and Bureau of Public Roads approve Mammoth Pass Road as FH 100 from North Fork to CA 203 in Mammoth Lakes. [DPW] [FBL].

1963: Position of Judge Ray Sherwin on "Mammoth Pass Road" summarized in February 21 newsletter. [SCB]

1964: President Johnson signs Wilderness Act on September 3. [WP]

1964: Mount Dana-Minarets Primitive Area now Minarets Wilderness Area. [CTL].

1964: Caltrans records 350,000 visitors to Mammoth Mountain Ski Area in 1964. [CTL]

1964: In a November 18 *Fresno Bee* story, B. F. Sisk first engages in road issue, studies geography and renames project Minaret Summit Road (MSR). Sisk recognizes the probable cost ($20 million) is beyond USFS budget and will need major federal grants. [FBL]

1965: On February 27, Congressman Sisk proposes all-weather hghway from North Fork to DPNM by way of Sheep's Crossing and Granite Stairway to be named Minaret Summit Highway. [CTL]

1965: Samuel B. Nelson cites name change from Mammoth Pass Road to Minaret Summit Road, following review of feasibility study. [DPW]

1965: BPR notifies CA Division of Highways that official name for proposed Mammoth Pass Road is Minaret Summit National Forest Highway. [CTL]

1965: April 23 *Fresno Bee* article "State Opens Bids to Study Sierra Road Link" is published. [FBL]

1965: On April 25, *Fresno Bee* publishes article "Sisk Backs Road to Link Rockies[sic]." [FBL]

1965: On June 11, Sierra Club announces opposition to any more trans-Sierra highways. [SCB] [CTL].

1965: On June 29, Calfornia Senate passes Joint Resolution 89 by senator J. A. Cobey and others, asking the Department of Public Works to study the feasibility of adding FH 100 to California Highway System and the interstate system, connecting I-5 to the Nevada border. [CTL]

1965: Lone Pine citizens oppose Minaret Pass Highway until Haiwee Pass Highway completed. [CTL]

1965: Mono County supervisor asks the State of California to include Minaret Highway in the California highway system. [CTL].

1965: Multiple *Fresno Bee* clippings on Congressman Sisk's efforts on behalf of Minaret Summet Road; Sisk asks FH 100 be added to California highway system and that I-70 be extended. [FBL]

1966: A January 26 letter is sent to Livermore from Walter Puhn of USFS regarding revisions to wilderness areas. Note the reference to USFS' role in diverting road consideration from Mammoth Pass and Lakes District. [GSP]

1966: California Division of Highways on March 25 reports Minaret Summit Highway too costly (estimated $125 million, plus $6.5 million annually for maintenance.) and recommends FH 100 not be added to state's responsibility. [CTL]

1966: Division of Highways report includes detail pertaining to I-70 extension from Cove Fort, Utah, across Nevada via US 6 to Benton Crossing, parallel to CA 120, over Crowley Lake via trestle to US 395, and through Mammoth Lakes. [CTL]

1966: According to Caltrans Library 203 chronology, Senate Transportation Committee learns interstate highway plan to be abandon in preference to a forty-mph all-year road CA 41 to US 395.

1966: On June 21, Assemblyman George Zenovich files Assembly Concurrent Resolution 41, seeking new feasibility study given new parameters. [CTL]

1966: Judge Ray Sherwin offers analysis of highway report. [SCB]

1966: California Division of Highways, in response to A.R. 41, submits in December a supplemental report, concluding road is still not feasible because of snow removal costs and insufficient traffic. Report ecommends FH 100 be excluded from California highway system. [CTL]

1967: Samuel Nelson sends letter to Senator Murphy refuting Mono County supervisor's belief that that all-year route cannot be maintained, only said it was not economically unfeasible. [CTL]

1967: California Division of Highways asks for $1.6 million in Public Lands Highway Funds along with $400,000 from the USFS to improve road access to Devils Postpile National Monument. [CTL]

1967: Zenovich and Ernest Mobley introduce Assembly Bill 290 to include FH 100 in California highway system. [CTL]

1967: Judge Sherwin and Genny Smith discuss second highway report in March *Sierra Club Bulletin*. [SCB]

1967: April 4 meeting of Transportation Committee Hearing on A.B. 290 postponed two weeks. [GSP]

1967: Sierra Club Wilderness Conference in San Francisco; Ike Livermore speaks at the conference and meets Genny Smith. [GSP]

1967: On April 9, a San Francisco Chronicle story reports that Livermore spoke out against Sierra Road, calling it a "tragedy." [SFC]

1967: Eastern Sierra Packers Association goes on the record as opposing Minarets Highway. [CTL]

1967: Letter from K. J. Grace of Pacific Intermountain Express to Genny Smith: Negative on road. [GSP]

1967: Snowy trip over Donner Summit on April 17 taken by Ervin and Beverly Van Nattan, Lou Roeser, and Doug Kittredge, bound for bill hearing. [CVI]

1967: Hearing for A.B. 290 occurred on April 18 at 10:30 a.m. in the Legislature Building. In addition to those mentioned above, also attending were Judge Ray Sherwin, Arch Mahan, and Lou and Dorothy Fitzhugh. [Dfl]

1967: In a Fresno Bee story on April 18, "Solons Kill Minaret Highway Bill," Congressman Sisk was critical of Livermore for testifying against the highway. The estimated cost for highway is now $200 million. [FBL].

1967: Livermore letter to Sherwin suggests new name—"John Muir Trail Association"—and is critical of Sierra Club ineffectiveness. [GSP]

1967: Sherwin writes on June 5, asking Charles Connaughton, Sheridan Farin and J. C. Womack to eliminate FH 100 from forest highway System [GSP]

1967: Genny Smith letter to Livermore on June 12 urges that he stimulate support from the Inyo County supervisor and business leaders. [GSP]

1967: July 21 letter from Trout Unlimited is critical of road. [GSP]

1967: Livermore hosts on-site study of corridor, departing September 17 with regional forester Jack Deinema and twenty others. [CTL]

1967: BPR's Sheridan Farin quoted as saying that "FH 100 is the most important unconstructed road in California." [CTL]

1967: S.B. 21 recommends acceptance into California Highway System CA 203 from Minaret Road to Minaret Summit. (diverting CA 203 from Horseshoe Lake). The bill was approved on November 8, 1967. [CTL].

1967: On November 21, the Mono County supervisor opposes Minaret Summit route as too costly and impractical. He favors some other trans-Sierra all-year highway. [CTL]

1967: On December 15, Judge Sherwin writes to Genny Smith a postscript on meeting with "Big 3": "Futile... all window dressing." [GSP].

1968: A February 18 letter from Ansel Adams urges compromise: Allow Minaret Summit Road in order to preclude any other roads. [GSP]

1968: On March 26, Mobley and Zenovich introduce A.B. 1191, essentially a rehash of A.B. 290 with no mention of the prior highway report. [CTL]

1968: A.B. 1191 hearings begin May 7. Livermore testifies against the bill. Strong opposition comes from Southern California, whose legislators want no more mileage in system that compete with their highways. Bill fails in Transportation Commission committee. [CTL]

1968: Assemblyman Eugene Chappie introduces H.R. 310 on June 20, which proposes that CA 108 over Sonora Pass be improved for year-round use. [CTL]

1970: In a May 5 story in the Fresno Bee, Fresno County business and civic leaders have not given up on support of thirty-one miles of road through state and federal lands. Sisk leads the effort in Washington, DC. [FBL]

1970: U.S. Secretary of Transportation writes that there are no plans to extend I-70 beyond Utah. [GSP]

1970: On November 15, Marilyn Hayden writes to Judge Sherwin, informing him of visual evidence of surveying on FH 100 down from Minaret Summit. [GSP]

1971: Genny Smith writes to Congressman Sisk, challenging his misrepresentation of FH 100 as already violating JMT. [GSP]

1971: On April 2, the Federal Highway Administration (formerly the BPR) issues environmental impact statement for FH 100 proposals; USFS and NPS have sought upgrade for years. Statement cites legislation introduced in the 91st Congress to designate the corridor as wilderness but that it was not reported out of committee. Yet. [CTL]

1972: On April 28, *Bridgeport Chronicle-Union* reports revised USFS stand on Minaret Road issue, which advises bifurcation of trans-Sierra highway from need for fixing road down to Devils Postpile. [BCU]

1972: On June 8, Secretary of Transportation Volpe replies to Governor Reagan and refuses to withdraw federal funding for FH100 improvements. [GSP]

1972: Break-in of Democratic National Committee headquarters at the Watergate Hotel occurs on June 17. [WP]

1972: Caspar Weinberger sends a memo to John Ehrlichman on June 22, asking for approval of wording for statement for use by Governor Reagan. On the same day, President Nixon first denies involvement in Watergate burglary attempt. [WP]

1972: A June 27 article in the *Fresno Bee* announces "Annual Ride Tomorrow," when "Governor . . . to inspect site of $2.7 million, 23-mile job site." [FBL]

1972: On June 28, the *Fresno Bee* via the McClatchy News Service (no FB reporters on ride?) Posted from Summit Meadow, Madera County, CA, the lead of the story read: "Gov. Reagan took to the saddle, rode three hours on six miles of trails." [FBL]

1972: June 29, FB – For subsequent reactions. [FBL]

1972: An August 8 letter from Ronald Reagan to US Senator Alan Cranston asks Cranston to support legislation to "permanently close minarets corridor." [GSP]

1972: On August 17, Sisk's letter to Reagan holds out for preservation of road corridor; a November reply refutes all of Sisk's arguments. [GSP]

1973: The California Division of Highways becomes the California Department of Transportation (Caltrans). [CTL]

1976: Genny Smith letter to Ike Livermore on Jan. 3 cites evidence of modest repairs to road extending to Reds Meadow Pack Station. [GSP]

1981: On July 17, California Congressman Phil Burton introduces H.R. 4083, which combines parts of H.R. 856 and H.R. 859; it was later resubmitted as H.R. 1437 [GSP]

1983: Fresno and Madera County efforts in support of corridor are revived. All of the old arguments are "taken out and dusted off": tungsten, national defense, and recreation. [FBL].

1983: On May 12, FHWA announces $2 million for an "escape route" (from seismic risk to Mammoth Lakes citizens); the editorial reaction in the *Fresno Bee* was "citizens of North Fork never offered their own escape route to east." [FBL]

1983: On April 12, H.R. 1437 (the "Burton Bill") passes House vote. [GSP]

1983: Burton Bill passes Senate vote on September 28. [GSP]

1984: A July 5 article in the *Fresno Bee* explains that the Cranston/Wilson wilderness bill would eliminate the corridor; Madera County supervisor Gordon Kennedy will ask fellow supervisors to voice opposition and seek compromise. [FBL]

1984: On July 7, the *Fresno Bee* reports that trans-Sierra backers are "girding for last-ditch battle to save corridor; progress of bill studied by all." The bill would set aside nineteen thousand acres of corridor as wilderness. Supervisor Kennedy is quoted as saying: "Might be 20 to 30 years before it's built; should keep corridor open." [FBL]

1984: On September 16, the Fresno Bee reports that "President Reagan will sign 'Omnibus California Wilderness Act'; sets aside 1.4 million acres for greater protection, including 110,000 acres to be named Ansel Adams Wilderness. [FBL]

1984: The California Wilderness Act of 1984 is signed into law on September 28; it is widely reported in California newspapers and conservation publications.

1985: On July 26, Genny Smith gives a speech to the Mono Lake Committee titled "Political Strategy: Ansel Adams Wilderness." The talk recalled her twenty-seven-year campaign and discussed "single-issue" advocacy. [GSP]

APPENDIX II

THE STORY RETOLD IN TWENTY DOCUMENTS

Author's Note:

MOST OF THE selected documents shown are self-explanatory.

Documents 9–12 document White House budget director Caspar Weinberger's solicitation of President Nixon's support, resulting in the initialed approval of assistant to the president John Ehrlichman for use of a presidential statement probably drafted by Weinberger. Whether any of this involved Nixon directly is not known.

Document 18 represents one of many hundreds of hand-drawn, hand-colored, and hand-copied maps distributed by Genny Smith as Congress deliberated the fate of the corridor and the final boundaries of what became the Ansel Adams Wilderness Area in 1984.

MONO COUNTY RESOURCES COMMITTEE
P.O. Box 701, Mammoth Lakes, California 93546

Robert Schotz, *President*
W. E. Van Nattan, *Vice-President*
Mrs. Marilyn Hayden, *Secretary-Treasurer*

Directors:
Tom Dempsey
Homer Elliott
Douglas Kittredge
Louis Roeser
Mrs. Genny Schumacher

The following business establishments support the Mono County Resources Committee as it 1) favors improving State Highway 108 over Sonora Pass to an all-year, all-weather route and 2) opposes construction of a Minaret Summit Highway, especially of the proposed Forest Highway 100:

Holiday Haus
International Inn
Mammoth Chevron Service
Ross Lodge and Youth Camp
Mammoth Trailer Rentals
Robert Hochenedel, accountant
Dempsey Construction Corporation
Tamarack Lodge
Crystal Crag Lodge
Lake Mary Store
Sierra Ready Mix
Mammoth Lakes Pack Outfit
Iron Horse Inn
Woods Lodge
Market Platz, Buster Norton
Reds Meadow Resort
Shell Station
Sam Basch Equipment
Associated Welding Company
Barker Auto Parts
Lloyd Nicoll, contractor
Don Zolnay, Mono Co. Plumbing Contrs.
Whites Lodge
Pine Cliff Resort

Kittredge Sporting Goods
Mammoth Building Material
Gribbon Equipment Rental
Kibbler Sheet Metal
Alpenrose Resort
Banner Lodge
Mammoth Laundromat
Mammoth Disposal
Sport Chalet
Willard Studio
Beets Formica Service
Stockwell's Delicatessen
Highlands Resort
Sierra Gables Resort
Ponderosa Lodge
Don Sharp
Meadows Electric
Frank's Plumbing Service
Sierra Pines Lodge
Tyrolean Lodge
Haddaway Manufacturing Company
Laurel Lodge
Edelweiss Lodge
Sierra Ice and Appliance Company
Bob Schotz, contractor

"Thoughtful Progress"

Why Should There Be A
MAMMOTH PASS ROAD?

THERE IS NO REAL REASON! Such a road does not serve defense needs — it must close t h r o u g h seven winter months. It has no commercial value; large rigs could not use it. It would rob existing roads of the funds they need for further development. It would cost the residents of its counties dearly for maintainence. And it would open no lakes, no specially distinctive areas for auto-tourist enjoyment.

SAY **NO** TO
BEER BOTTLES
and BULLDOZERS

And Why There Should NOT Be!

This Would Be

DESTRUCTION
–NOT PROGRESS!

There are all too few truly wild areas left for this generation and others to come to enjoy. This road bisects famed Muir Trail as well as the Mt. Dana-Minarets and High Sierra Wild Areas. Its most scenic areas are already available on existing roads; it is a land made to be enjoyed by those who love wilderness country.

Even now, there are not enough funds to permit the Forest Service to clean up after the litterbugs. Why risk still another area to permanent destruction of wilderness beauty?

Join the fight now against the beer can brigade! Close the corridor between Minarets and High Sierra Wilderness areas to all such roads forever!

Write YOUR
Congressman . . . Assemblyman . . . Senator . . . . . . Regional Forester

TODAY
ENJOY THE WILDERNESS TOMORROW!

Who supports the road?

The leading proponents of the road are found in the Madera Chamber of Commerce. They are supported by the Mono and Bishop Chambers of Commerce and the Madera and Mono Boards of Supervisors. In 1959, the Mammoth Lakes Chamber of Commerce and the Mono Supervisors asked for an all year highway and apparently split with the Madera County groups which were supporting any kind of a road.

Who opposes the road?

Central California Sportsmen's Council

Sierra Natural Resources Committee

Western Unit of High Sierra
  Packers Association

Sierra Club

California Garden Clubs

105 Mammoth Lakes property owners

National Campers & Hikers Association

Kern County Fish and Game
  Protective Association

Federation of Western Outdoor Clubs

California Wildlife Federation

American Nature Association

Tuesday Club of Kingsburg

Commonwealth Club

1,304 Mammoth Lakes residents and
  visitors by 1959 petition

National Parks Association

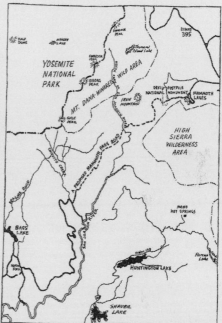

The dotted line shows the general location of the several proposed routes for the Mammoth Pass Road. Any such route would effectively sever the longest — and one of the finest — stretches of wilderness left intact in the United States.

Minimum Bureau of Public Roads estimate on a Mammoth Pass road now stands at $19,245,000 for 82.9 miles of road. The bureau reports that the road is feasible, that the road can be justified economically. The real questions, however, is: Can a better use be made of the nearly $20 million?

San Francisco Chronicle:

"New Trans-Sierra road is last thing we need."

CALIFORNIA LEGISLATURE—1967 REGULAR SESSION

ASSEMBLY BILL   No. 290

Introduced by Assemblymen Zenovich, Mobley, Murphy, Milias, Badham, Bagley, Chappie, Duffy, Ketchum, MacDonald, Monagan, Pattee, Shoemaker, and Veneman
(Senators Way, Burns, and Short, coauthors)

January 31, 1967

REFERRED TO COMMITTEE ON TRANSPORTATION AND COMMERCE

An act to amend Section 452 of the Streets and Highways Code, relating to state highway routes.

The people of the State of California do enact as follows:

1   SECTION 1. Section 452 of the Streets and Highways Code
2 is amended to read:
3   452. Route 152 is from:
4   (a) Route 1 near Watsonville to Route 101 via Hecker
5 Pass.
6   (b) Route 101 to Route 65 near Sharon via Pacheco Pass.
7   *(c) Route 41 near Yosemite National Park to Route 395 via*
8 *North Fork and Minaret Summit.*

LEGISLATIVE COUNSEL'S DIGEST

AB 290, as introduced, Zenovich (Trans. & C.). State highway routes.
Amends Sec. 452, S. & H.C.
Extends Route 152 from Route 41 near Yosemite National Park to Route 395 via North Fork and Minaret Summit.
Vote—Majority; Appropriation—No; State Expense—Yes.

FACT SHEET

PREFACE

When the Secretary of Agriculture established the High Sierra Wilderness (now known as the John Muir Wilderness,) and the Dana-Minaret Wilderness, a narrow corridor was left between for a trans-Sierra Highway from Madera County over Minaret Summit to Mono County, if and when needed. There has been controversy since over whether the road was necessary and desirable or whether the corridor area should be incorporated into the adjacent wilderness.

These are the proponent's arguments and the facts.

The proponents of the road have made the following contentions:

1. ARGUMENT

The road was first proposed as a defense highway.

FACT

The Army Chief of Staff and Commanding General of the area announced that the road was not necessary for defense purposes.

2. ARGUMENT

The road was proposed as a means of access for lumbering.

FACT

The U. S. Forest Service has stated that no extensions of existing roads were necessary to tap commercially valuable timber.

3. ARGUMENT

The road was proposed as a means of access to minerals.

FACT

No mineral deposits in the area are of sufficient quantity or quality to warrant commercial development.

4. ARGUMENT

The road was proposed as a means of exporting San Joaquin Valley Agricultural and manufactured products.

FACT

The State Division of Highways has reported that no highway suitable for this kind of traffic was economically feasible because of excessive costs of construction and maintenance over rugged terrain and high altitudes and further by reason of excessive costs of snow removal.

5. ARGUMENT

The road has been justified primarily by reason of expected traffic to winter sports areas.

FACT

The same feasibility s t u d y which charted winter sports traffic as the single greatest potential use, introduced its report on the Mammoth Pass route corridor with the remark that "There are few possible routes through the rugged, rocky terrain and that none can be expected to provide for year round traffic."

CALIFORNIA LEGISLATURE—1968 REGULAR SESSION

ASSEMBLY BILL   No. 1191

Introduced by Assemblymen Mobley and Zenovich
(Coauthors: Senators Burns and Way)

March 26, 1968

REFERRED TO COMMITTEE ON TRANSPORTATION AND COMMERCE

*An act to amend Section 503 of the Streets and Highways
Code, relating to State Highway Route 203.*

The people of the State of California do enact as follows:

1   SECTION 1.   Section 503 of the Streets and Highways Code
2 is amended to read:
3   503.   Route 203 is from :
4   *(a) Route 41 near San Joaquin Experimental Range to the*
5 *Mono county line near Minaret Summit.*
6   *(b)* The Mono county line near Minaret Summit to Route
7 395.
8   *The commission may allocate from the State Highway Fund*
9 *the necessary funds for the acquisition of right-of-way and*
10 *construction of all or any portion of section (a) of said route*
11 *as funds are available. If, however, said funds cannot be pro-*
12 *grammed for the completion of the central portion of the route,*
13 *between the vicinity of Sheep Crossing and southerly of the*
14 *Devils Postpile, within a reasonable period of time, the com-*
15 *mission is authorized to investigate and report to the Legisla-*
16 *ture on the feasibility of accelerating the construction of all or*
17 *a part of said central portion by other means, including use*
18 *charges or tolls.*

LEGISLATIVE COUNSEL'S DIGEST

AB 1191, as introduced, Mobley (Trans. & C.). State Highways—
Route 203.

Amends Sec. 503, S. & H.C.

Adds to Route 203, a portion from Route 41 near the San Joaquin
Experimental Range to the Mono county line near Minaret Summit.
Authorizes the California Highway Commission to investigate feasibility
of use charges or tolls if funds are not available within a reasonable
time for construction of the central portion of this route between the
vicinity of Sheep Crossing and southerly of Devils Postpile.

Vote—Majority; Appropriation—No; Fiscal Committee—Yes.

O

BONNER PACKING COMPANY

64 No. Fulton St.' Phone (209) 268-5731 Cable BOPACO P.O. Box 2072

FRESNO, CALIFORNIA 95718

April 24, 1968

Mr. Norman Livermore, Administrator
Resources Agency
1416 Ninth St.
Sacramento, California

Dear Mr. Livermore:

You have asked us as a shipper of dried fruits from central
California if a new road over the Minarets Summit would be
an advantage in getting our product to market. I can cate-
gorically state that it would have no appreciable advantage,
and any persons stating otherwise are making claims that are
extremely far-fetched. To be more specific, our firm, the
Bonner Packing Company, processes and ships about 10% of the
raisins from the Fresno area. Our experience, therefore,
would be more or less representative of the entire industry,
which ships a total of approximately 230,000 tons a year.
Actually in the last 12 months our firm shipped 26,000 tons
as follows: 2,000 tons went to Canada by railroad or truck,
7,000 tons went overseas by truck to the Port of Stockton,
2,000 tons went intrastate to either Los Angeles or San Francisco
area, 8,000 tons went by railroad to eastern markets, and
7,000 tons went by truck to eastern markets. These trucks
carry about 17 tons; therefore, about 400 trucks a year leave
our plant in Fresno to go east.

Most of these trucks are loaded in more than one place and are
known as pool trucks. Anyway, if the cargo is destined for
Chicago or the Middlewest area, it will be first loaded here;
and then the load will be completed in San Jose. Obviously
the truck will go east over the Donner Summit. If the load is
going to the Eastern Seaboard, it is first loaded in San Jose
and completed here in Fresno and then goes over the Tehachapi
Summit out of Bakersfield to connect with Highway 66.

As far as we can see, if there was a Minarets Summit Road, there
would be no advantage whatsoever because the same truck, after
crossing the summit, would have to either go north or south
on the Nevada side to connect either with Highway 40 or Highway 66.

In conclusion, I might add that we did not entirely trust our
own judgment in this matter and have conferred with the Truck
Dispatch Company here in Fresno who dispatches thousands of
trucks out of this area. They totally agree with the thoughts
expressed in this letter; and, in fact, both of us as taxpayers
would strongly object to our money being spent for a needless
road of this type.

Yours sincerely

CHARLES W. BONNER
President

CWB/th

by Ansel Adams in *This Is the American Earth*

SIERRA CLUB   Mills Tower, San Francisco 94104

August 14, 1969

Lou Roesser
Mammoth Lakes, Calif.

Dear Mr. Roesser:

Once again we are faced with the challenge of the Minaret Summit road. This year the scheme is wrapped up in a supposedly less offensive proposal to build an access road to the Devils Postpile area. It does not take much imagination to see that the completion of this seven mile section of road will in future years lead to increased agitation for the entire trans-Sierran route. I hope that you will join in an effort to stop this road.

The Federal Highway Administration is holding hearings at the Mammoth Lakes Visitors Center on August 20 at 10 A.M. If it is at all possible for you to be present, your testimony could do immeasurable good. If you cannot get to Mammoth Lakes, written testimony will also be accepted. Statements should be sent to the Federal Highway Admin- istration, 450 Golden Gate Avenue, Box 36090, San Francisco, California 94102. The deadline for written testimony is August 30.

One word of caution. Apparently the position of the FHA is that discussion of the Trans-Sierra route is not pertinent to the consideration of this year's restricted project, and thus is not admissible in test- imony. Comment, either oral or written, should be directed primarily to the first segment of the proposal: the access route into the Postpiles area.

I hope that the enclosed position paper will be of assistance to any effort you wish to make. If you have further questions, please get in touch with Mr. Jonathan Ela at the Sierra Club, 1050 Mills Tower, San Francisco, Calif. 94104. The telephone there is 981-8634.

Thank you very much for giving this matter your attention. I appreciate any action you can take to help stop this misguided proposal.

Sincerely,

Raymond J. Sherwin

RJS/sm

EXECUTIVE
HI2/ST3 ⁹
PR14-8
ST5
FG6-16
Trans-Sierra
Minarets

EXECUTIVE OFFICE OF THE PRESIDENT
OFFICE OF MANAGEMENT AND BUDGET
WASHINGTON, D.C. 20503

June 22, 1972

MEMORANDUM FOR JOHN EHRLICHMAN

Attached is a statement by the President, which the
Governor of California has been authorized to release
in California next week in accordance with the
decision you gave me on June 21, 1972.

Caspar W. Weinberger

Attachment

cc: Ron Ziegler
    Bob Haldeman
    John Mitchell
    Clark MacGregor
    Secretary Volpe
    Secretary Butz
    Bill Gifford
    Bill Morrill
    John Whitaker

4/21

MEMORANDUM FOR JOHN EHRLICHMAN

The California Minarets position is as follows:

DOT (Beggs) has reluctantly agreed to the decision
outlined in the attached proposed Presidential
statement.

Secretary Butz (on behalf of the Forest Service) also
has no objection.

Governor Reagan and the various State political types
feel very strongly that the President should be
positioned in accordance with the attached statement,
and that it should be available for the Governor to
use as soon as possible. The Sierra Club plans to
hold a press conference at the Minarets site on June 28,
which initially had been called for the purpose of
attacking the Administration because of the earlier
Volpe decision to reconstruct part of the Minarets
Highway and DOT's refusal to state that the Trans-
Sierra Highway would not be built.

There are at least two appropriate alternatives for
use of the statement.

1) Secretary Morton is visiting the Governor next week
and the statement could be used as an announcement at
the Minarets press conference, and thus turn the whole
thing into a celebration for the Administration's
forthright stand. Although Interior is not directly
involved, Secretary Morton's visit would tie in nicely
with the conservationists support for this position.
2) The Governor and Secretary Morton could announce it
jointly at a Sacramento press conference prior to June 28.

-2-

Numerous other alternatives are undoubtedly possible.
The main thing now is speed so we can confirm to
California, and incidentally solidify, the
Administration's position as outlined in the attached
statement.

No problem

Do you have any problem with my advising the Governor's
office that the statement does represent the
Administration's position?

yes

Should it be released in connection with Secretary
Morton's trip?

I would appreciate your advice as soon as possible.

Caspar W. Weinberger

cc: Ron Ziegler
     John Mitchell
     John Whitaker

AUTHOR'S NOTE: Initialed approval in margin comes from assistant to
the president John Ehrlichman. Whether any of this involved President
Nixon directly is not known.

PRESIDENTIAL STATEMENT

MINARETS HIGHWAY — TRANS-SIERRA HIGHWAY

The President announced today that the proposed reconstruction of a portion of the Minarets Highway in California will not be undertaken, and the proposed Trans-Sierra Highway (Forest Highway 100) will not be built.

The President said he agreed with the recommendations of Governor Reagan of California that damage would be done to the environment by the reconstruction of a portion of the existing highway, and by the construction of long proposed Trans-Sierra Highway. The President said that the environmental considerations and the need to preserve the atmosphere and ecology of the Sierra region of California clearly overrode the other factors that had been urged in supporting the construction proposals.

RED'S MEADOW TIMES

RESORT AND PACK STATIONS

| First Edition | Red's Meadow | Mammoth Lakes, California 93546 | Inyo National Forest | Summer 1973 |

PRESIDENT RICHARD NIXON STOPS TRANS-SIERRA HIGHWAY

Plan Your Pack Trip Vacation

Have you ever had the desire to get away from it all? Fascinating scenery — serenity —adventures in fishing, photography, camping, riding, climbing and hunting are all easily available on your pack trip of a lifetime.

Red's Meadow Pack Stations offers suggestions and assistance in planning your pack trip so that you may enjoy this wonderful experience to the fullest.

Maps, brochures, menus, suggested areas, and check lists of personal items and camp gear are all available upon request. Red's Meadow Pack Station has been providing service and assisting parties plan pack trips for the past 37 years. Our justification for existence is to be of service to you. Leave some problems for us—so far we've packed everything that has been brought to us — from kids to helicopters.

Red's Meadow offers a
(Continued on Page 2)

GOVERNOR REAGAN DEPARTS ON HISTORICAL PACK TRIP ON LADY

MULE HOUSE CAFE

Perhaps you've heard about a tough steak—wait'll you try a Muleburger— Packer's Special Trail Rider's Delight — Over-the-Falls Upside Down Cake!

Along with the renowned specialties of the menu of the Mule House Cafe is a collection of pictures of some of the celebrated and interesting guests of Red's Meadows, as well as a pictorial history of Red's Meadow, which now adorn the walls of the Mule House Cafe.

Jim and Hazel Bivens of Huntington Park have assisted the collection with the donation of portraits of Anacleto Torres and Curt Goin. Torres packed for Red's Meadow from 1944 through 1968 until his death at the age of 92. He, no doubt, had the most famous and notorious string of white mules in the history of the Sierra. Curt was a packer and stagecoach driver from 1938 through 1963. Both are well remembered by their many friends.

The Bivens also contributed a fine reproduction of western artist Charles Russell's **A Tight Dally and a Loose Latigo**.

A pictorial history of Governor Ronald Reagan's pack trip and unprecedented press conference is displayed in a massive collage.

We invite you to come browse around the Mule House Cafe. By the way, the food isn't too bad, either—the Red's Meadow crew and family has been enjoying it since 1934. (Some wit at the dinner table just suggested that the cook's stew was of the same vintage.)

Wilderness Permits

Wilderness permits for pack trip guests available at Agnew Meadows and Red's Meadow Pack Stations.

Gov. Reagan Announces President's Decision On Trans-Sierra Highway While On Red's Meadow Pack Trip

One hundred head of pack and saddle stock accompanied Governor Reagan for an unprecedented press conference to announce the President's decision to withhold $2.7 million for road improvement on the proposed Trans-Sierra Highway.

In one of the great environmental decisions of the decade, the funds for construction of the first phase of the Trans-Sierra Highway from Minaret Summit to Agnew Meadows was withdrawn by Executive Order in June of 1972.

Of equal significance is the Governor's announcement that the State of California will support legislation to join the John Muir and Minaret Wilderness Areas and thereby eliminate the possibility of a Trans-Sierra Highway through Red's Meadow.

RAINBOW FALLS

DEVIL'S POSTPILE NATIONAL MONUMENT

Family Fun • Mother's Delight • Father's Dream • Children's Paradise

State of California
GOVERNOR'S OFFICE
SACRAMENTO 95814

RONALD REAGAN
GOVERNOR

July 24, 1972

Mr. Bob Tanner
Red's Meadow Resort
Mammoth Lakes, California

Dear Bob:

Mere words are inadequate to express my thanks
to you and your wife for the hours of preliminary
work and hurculean effort necessary to gather
together the number of riding and pack horses
required to move the persons involved in the
Minarets - Forest Highway 100 ride. You both
did an outstanding job in an almost impossible
situation.

And, by the way, I want to also thank you for
the excellent horse provided for my use. As I
recall, her name is "Lady", as indeed she is.
Please give her my regards.

All this combined to make the entire affair a
real pleasure. It will be, for me, an event to
long remember.

Sincerely,

Ronald Reagan

RONALD REAGAN
Governor

State of California

GOVERNOR'S OFFICE
SACRAMENTO 95814

RONALD REAGAN
GOVERNOR

July 24, 1972

Mrs. Ward C. Smith
P. O. Box 1068
Mammoth Lakes, California 93546

Dear Mrs. Smith:

Sometimes the going gets pretty rugged here in
Sacramento, as you can well imagine. It is
certainly fortifying to be reminded that we have
the support of a great many concerned citizens
as we face the challenges of governing California.

I am very grateful for your words of encouragement
and hope I will continue to merit your confidence.

Sincerely,

RONALD REAGAN
Governor

THE SECRETARY OF HEALTH, EDUCATION, AND WELFARE
WASHINGTON, D. C. 20201

MAR 20 1973

Mrs. Ward C. Smith
1304 Pitman Avenue
Palo Alto, California 94301

Dear Mrs. Smith:

Many thanks for your letter enclosing a copy of
your message to the President about budget
priorities. I appreciate hearing your views on
this subject.

It was very thoughtful of you to write about my
opposition to the Trans-Sierra road. I share
your concern about the California wilderness and
am glad to do what I can to help save it.

Thank you again for writing.

Sincerely,

Secretary

San Joaquin Wilderness Association

Post Office Box 9856 • Fresno, California 93794

THE SAN JOAQUIN WILDERNESS NEEDS YOUR HELP!

Founding Members

Raymond Sherwin

Harold E. Thomas

Advisory Council

Tony Chasteen
Sebastopol

Lynne Foster
Mammoth Lakes

August Fruge
Twentynine Palms

Bob Gray
San Diego

Doug Harwell
Fresno

Rich Kangas
Selma

Andrea Lawrence
Mammoth Lakes

Martin Litton
Portola Valley

Norman B. Livermore, Jr.
San Rafael

John Modin
El Dorado Hills

Margaret Molarsky
Ross

Gary Schroeder
Fresno

Genny Smith
Mammoth Lakes

Beverly Steveson
Bakersfield

George Whitmore
Fresno

The Wilderness

The proposed San Joaquin Wilderness lies along the crest of the central Sierra Nevada. Diverse in character, it ranges from the 3000-foot deep granite gorge of the San Joaquin River to snowy Iron Mountain, its forests interspersed with picturesque volcanic outcrops and lush meadows. Although crossed by the John Muir and Pacific Crest trails, much of this area is lightly used because of topographic barriers and primitive trailhead access. Its isolation and middle elevation provide a haven for many wildlife species. The northern portion of this beautiful area was once (until 1905) part of Yosemite National Park.

For many years Madera County has viewed this de facto wilderness as a potential trans-Sierra highway route, which would sever the John Muir Trail as well as the longest contiguous wilderness in the lower 48 states. The threat of highway construction is still alive and will remain until wilderness is established. Happily, the San Joaquin Wilderness is included in the California Wilderness Bill (HR 1437) which was just approved by the U.S. House of Representatives.

The Compromises

The San Joaquin Roadless Area (5-047) inventoried by the U.S. Forest Service contained 159,000 acres. During the past six years all competing interests have taken part in drawing the boundaries. All of the areas east of the Sierra crest were excluded from wilderness to accommodate more downhill ski areas. A site for a diversion dam on the North Fork of the San Joaquin was included to accommodate hydroelectric interests. Road access accommodates the cattle grazing permittee. Large tracts west of the Green Mountain-Cattle Mountain divide and another west of the South Fork were excluded from wilderness to accommodate lumber industry demands. The resulting proposal contains only 110,000 acres.

YOSEMITE NATIONAL PARK

MINARETS WILDERNESS

JOHN MUIR WILDERNESS

SAN JOAQUIN ROADLESS AREA

SEQUOIA-KINGS CANYON NATIONAL PARK

Save The John Muir Trail

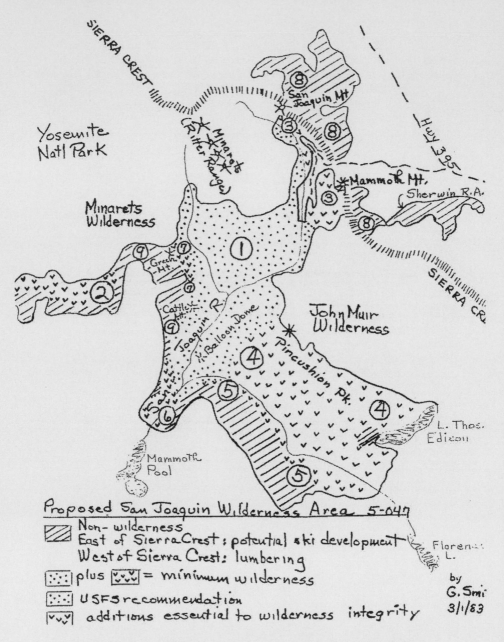

Proposed San Joaquin Wilderness Area 5-047

▨ Non-wilderness
East of Sierra Crest: potential ski development
West of Sierra Crest: lumbering

▦ plus ⱽⱽⱽ = minimum wilderness

▦ USFS recommendation

ⱽⱽⱽ additions essential to wilderness integrity

by
G. Smi
3/1/83

AUTHOR'S NOTE: This is one of many hundreds of hand-drawn, hand-colored, and hand-copied maps distributed by Genny Smith while Congress deliberated the fate of the corridor and the final boundaries of what became the Ansel Adams Wilderness Area in 1984.

RICHARD H. LEHMAN
18TH DISTRICT, CALIFORNIA

1319 LONGWORTH BUILDING
WASHINGTON, D.C. 20515
(202) 225-4540

COMMITTEE ON
BANKING, FINANCE AND
URBAN AFFAIRS

COMMITTEE ON
INTERIOR AND INSULAR
AFFAIRS

Congress of the United States
House of Representatives
Washington, D.C. 20515
September 17, 1984

Ward and Genny Smith
Post Office Box 1060
Mammoth Lakes, California 93546

Dear Ward and Genny:

September 12, 1984 was a landmark day for all Californians,
and I am particularly pleased to share the good news with you
in light of your support for legislation to create a Mono Basin
National Forest Scenic Area. In addition to setting aside 1.8
million acres of wilderness and designating the Tuolumne River as
Wild and Scenic, final House passage of H.R. 1437, the Omnibus
California Conservation Bill, included all major portions of my
bill to provide national recognition for Mono Lake.

Because you have expressed interest in Mono Lake in the past,
I have enclosed an excerpt from the debate on the final passage of
H.R. 1437 to share with you a sense of this historic event. With
Presidential signature of this bill, protection of the gem of the
Eastern Sierras will at long last become a reality.

I am grateful for your support in this endeavor.

Sincerely,

RICHARD H. LEHMAN
Member of Congress

RHL/mc

Please Respond to:

WASHINGTON OFFICE

FRESNO OFFICE
1900 MARIPOSA MALL
SUITE 301
FRESNO, CALIFORNIA 93721
(209) 487 5760

STOCKTON OFFICE
808 NORTH CENTER STREET
STOCKTON, CALIFORNIA 95202
(209) 946-6353

SONORA OFFICE
9 NORTH WASHINGTON STREET
SONORA, CALIFORNIA 95370
(209) 533-1426

SIERRA CLUB

CA/NV Representative
6014 College Ave., Oakland, CA 94618 (415) 654-7847
October 15, 1984

TO WILDERNESS ACTIVISTS

Dear Friend,

There was no ceremony, not even a press release from the White House, but President Reagan signed the California Wilderness Act into law on September 28th. Congratulations!

--The Forest Service will now figure out how to implement wilderness management on the new areas. They completed final maps of the new areas (done from the House committee maps), but won't publish them for some time.

--Areas still in further planning are protected at least until their Forest Plan is finalized. Three "planning areas" are protected for 4 years. Everything else not designated wilderness is "released."

--A wilderness EIS is no longer needed before timber sales or other activities can proceed in "released" areas. Defending these areas will be difficult. It will have to be done on the basis of local, site specific issues other than wilderness. We will need to concentrate on areas that are truly high priorities, and realistically assess whether we have or can create the volunteer effort and expertise needed to save an area.

--There have been successful defenses of areas not using wilderness issues. The Blue Creek area of the Siskiyous is one of the best examples. Appeals and a lawsuit challenged the Forest Service's environmental documentation, the rationale of their development decisions, and conflicts with environmental (and other) laws. The court stopped development.

--Plugging the new wilderness areas into the forest plans requires new computer runs, delaying draft plans for most timbered forests 6-9 months.

--Zane Smith's direction to the forests for '85-'90 places strong emphasis on improving wilderness management.

--Congress passed timber contract relief legislation. Loggers can buy out of 55% of the volume of their contracts. They pay $10/MBF to 30% of the bid price, depending on the size of the company. Freed-up sales will be resold as part of, and not in addition to, the normal timber sales program, and will be given preference in the sales program.

--Asst. Secretary of Agriculture John Crowell is leaving his post after the election. Rumours as to successors abound.

--Thanks to Bob Kanne for writing a letter published by the L.A. Times about wilderness after the bill passed. The next wilderness battle starts now!

Sincerely yours,

Russ Shay

SOURCE NOTES

Prologue

1 "Roads to Somewhere: the highways that have changed America's social and economic face," *The Economist*, June 24, 2006, 36–37.

2 "Why Should There Be A Mammoth Pass Road?" Fact sheet prepared by W. E. Van Nattan, Mono County Resources Committee, Mammoth Lakes, CA, 1968.

3 From the north, Feather River Highway (CA 70), CA 49, Donner Summit (I-80), Echo Summit (US 50), Carson Pass (CA 88), Ebbetts Pass (CA 4), Sonora Pass (CA 108), Tioga Pass (CA 120), Walker Pass (CA 178), Tehachapi Pass (CA 58), according to Caltrans.

Chapter 1, Roads Running Wild

4 Norman B. Livermore Jr., "Roads Running Wild," *American Forests*, April 1938.

5 Remnants of this 1929 road can be seen from a hiking trail that descends from Minaret Summit to Starkweather Lake. The current road is its functional replacement; Ike Livermore recalled the story of his camping trip to Pumice flats in "Man in the Middle," an oral history conducted for the Sierra Club by the Univesity of California Bancroft Library in 1983.

6 Norman Livermore interviewed at his home in San Rafael, CA, in 2006 and 2007.

7 N. B. Livermore Jr., Remarks at Commonwealth Club Symposium, "Should We Stop Building New Roads into California's High Mountains," June 2, 1936.

8 Prior to the Wilderness Act of 1964, USFS designated certain forests within its jurisdiction as "primitive areas," for example the Dana-Minarets Primitive Area, later to become the Minarets Wilderness.

9 N. B. Livermore Jr., "Packing in 50 Years Ago," *The Album: Times and Tales of Inyo-Mono County*, Chalfant Press, July 1990.

10 Documents outlining parameters of this road proposal held by Caltrans Archives, Sacramento, CA.

11 Virginia Livermore joined us for both interviews and generously contributed her fond memories.

12 News Release–State of California Dept. Public Works, February 9, 1966: "Improvements to the Eastern End of Tioga Pass Road," for publication in *California Highways and Public Works Magazine*, January–February 1966.

13 Caltrans Archives, Sacramento, folder on CA 203.

14 "Maderans Back Northfork to Nevada Route," *Fresno Bee*, February 19, 1939; In 1980, the Hawthorne facility was transferred from navy to army jurisdiction and is now under the management of a private contractor. (see http://www.globalsecurity.org).

15 "Highway Over Sierra Sought As Defense Project," *Fresno Bee*, August 24, 1941; Alaska would suffer the nation's only wartime troop invasion, limited to the remote Aleutian Islands of Attu and Kiska.

Chapter 2, Early Sierra Crossings

16 Thomas Frederick Howard, *Sierra Crossings: First Roads to California* (Berkeley: University of California Press, 1998), 23.

17 Mary Hill, *Geology of the Sierra Nevada* (Berkeley, University of California Press, 2006) 179–86; John McPhee, *Assembling California* (New York: Farrar, Straus, and Giroux, 1993), 28–30.

18 R. F. Heizer and M. A. Whipple, *The California Indians: A Source Book* (Berkeley, University of California Press, 1971).

19 Mono Paiute elder and retired American Airlines pilot Alan Blaver, who joins these treks each summer, was interviewed in 2009. He spoke from the heart about of the importance of demonstrating unity and identity with Native Americans living in the area.

20 Francis P. Farquhar, *History of the Sierra Nevada*, (Berkeley: University of California Press, 1965), 15.

21 Cited by Howard, *Sierra Crossing: First Roads to California*, 15–18.

22 Ibid.,17–23.

23 Ibid., 20.

24 Ibid., 23–35.

25 Charles F. McGlashan, *History of the Donner Party: A Tragedy of the Sierra,* (New York: Barnes & Noble, 2004), 194-195.

26 Marshall Fey, R. Joe King, Jack Lepisto, *Emigrant Shadows: A History and Guide to the California Trail* (Virginia City, NV: Western Trails Research Association, 2002), 21–49, 110–12.

27 Kevin Starr, *California: A History* (New York: Modern Library, 2005), 79–90.

28 Richard White, *Railroaded: The Transcontinentals and the Making of Modern America* (New York: W. W. Norton, 2011); Howard, *Sierra Crossing.*

Chapter 3, Destination Resort

29 Douglas Kittredge to Walter Powell, June 29, 1967; Chip Van Nattan interviewed in 2008.

30 Adele Reed, *Old Mammoth* (Palo Alto, CA: Genny Smith Books, 1982).

31 Gary Caldwell, *Mammoth Gold: The Ghost Towns of Lake District* (Mammoth Lakes, CA: Genny Smith Books, 1990).

32 Plaque on a stone marker at former Mammoth City site indicates that there were twenty-two saloons, thirteen stores, two breweries, two livery stables, five restaurants, and two newspapers (no mention of the brothels that surely functioned).

33 These meadowlands have been renamed, often according to their owner at the time. According to Marye Roeser, the lower meadow near Laurel and Sherwin Creeks has been referred to as Rawson Meadow, then Summers Meadow, and finally Laurel Meadow. The main meadow was called Mammoth Meadow, then after 1938 Old Mammoth Meadow, and later Arcularious Meadow. The upper meadow was sometimes called Hidden Lake Meadow. The mountains above the meadow were not named for Sherwin (as in Sherwin Bowl) until developers proposed a ski area for these slopes, which hasn't happened nor is it likely as of this writing.

34 Cited by Adele Reed in *Old Mammoth,* 43; according to Reed, the Wildasinn Hotel first opened for guests in 1906.

35 It was also designated a component of the "Three flags Highway," combining the routes of several highways extending from Mexico through several Western states into Canada. Refer to Caltrans Archive under folder for CA 395.

36 When this road was extended to Horseshoe Lake and became State Route 112, its name for a time was Mammoth Lakes Road, but it never stuck with locals who still refer to Lake Mary Road.

37 Adele Reed's *Old Mammoth* is a valuable reference for photographs of the village at the time roads were changing and new structures were appearing; Lloyd Wilson recalled for me how mail was received and distributed.

38 Robin Morning, *Tracks of Passion: Eastern Sierra Skiing, Dave McCoy, and Mammoth Mountain,* (Mammoth Lakes, CA: Mammoth Lakes Foundation, 2008).

39 WPA: Works Progress Administration, the largest of President Roosevelt's New Deal organizations, was established in 1935.

40 1946 USFS ski survey cited in Robin Morning, *Tracks of Passion,* 143.

41 "Road is Needed," *Fresno Bee,* June 18, 1946.

42 The M29 Weasel was designed by the British for use on snow and manufactured by Studebaker in South Bend, Indiana. They were eventually used in Europe and in the Pacific under muddy conditions that immobilized wheeled vehicles.

43 David R. Brower, Statement before Joint Meeting of the Fresno and Madera County Supervisors, Fresno, April 20, 1956.

44 "Supervisors See Need to Extend Mammoth Road," *Fresno Bee,* August 15, 1953.

45 Editorial appearing in the *Fresno Bee,* September 5, 1956.

46 "Opponents of Mammoth Road Name Officers," *Fresno Bee,* July 23, 1957; "New Sierra Highway Faces Nature Lovers' Opposition," *San Francisco Examiner,* October 20, 1957.

Chapter 4 "Dear People, Start Writing Letters."

47 Letter from Genny Schumacher, her married name at the time, written on December 5, 1958. For clarity and currency she is referred to as Genny Smith throughout this book.

48 "Trans-Sierra Highway Plan Said Feasible," *Bakersfield Californian*, November 19, 1958.

49 "Mammoth Pass Road Backed by U.S. Agency," *Fresno Bee*. Nov. 18, 1958.

50 Mimeography or stencil duplication was used before xerography was popularized in the 1960s; Genny Smith recalled for me Mr. Farin's reaction to the deluge of letters.

51 Genny Smith was interviewed too many times to recount. Her assistance and her papers, some held privately and others given to the Bancroft Library, were invaluable.

52 Genny Smith interview.

53 Lou and Marye Roeser were interviewed for this book many times; Dorothy Fitzhugh recalled for me activities of the Mono County Resources Committee.

54 Alan H. Patera, *Bennettville and the Tioga Mining District*, Western Places Monograph Series, No. 25, 2003.

55 "Justice Douglas Opposes Highway," *Fresno Bee*, September 15, 1959.

56 "Sierra Club Reaffirms Stand Against MPR," *Fresno Bee*, September 29, 1959; "FCC Seeks All Year Sierra Road," *Fresno Bee*, December 16, 1959.

57 *Fresno Bee*, January 8, 1960.

58 Notes from this meeting in Genny Smith Papers, Bancroft Library, University of California–Berkeley, Box 1.

59 See B. F. Sisk in http://www.PoliticalGraveyard.com.

60 "Congressman B.F. Sisk Asks for Speed-up of Route Studies," *Fresno Bee*, November 18, 1964.

61 CA 203 Chronology, Caltrans Library, Sacramento, CA.

62 "Sisk Backs Road to Link Rockies With Valley," *Fresno Bee*, April 25, 1965.

63 B. F. Sisk press release reported by the McClatchey Newspaper Service, February 2, 1965.

64 Ray Sherwin essay describing his journey along the proposed route: "Minaret Summit to North Fork: Wilderness or Trans-Sierra Highway," 1966, Genny Smith Papers, Bancroft Library, University of California, Berkeley, CA.

65 Judge Ray Sherwin, "Mammoth Pass Road Newsletter," February 21, 1963.

Chapter 5 Highways of History

66 Geoffrey Hindley, *A History of Roads* (London: Peter Davies, 1971), 1–6.

67 Ibid., 19.

68 ibid., 21–24.

69 Ibid., 30–40.

70 Ibid., 12–16.

71 Ian Frazier, "Travels in Siberia: The Ultimate Road Trip," *New Yorker,* August 3, 2009.

72 Hindley, *A History of Roads*, 4, 74, 77–78.

73 Ibid., 60–63.

74 Ibid., 4, 80–82.

75 Third Avenue in Manhattan was the first street to be paved using the "Macadam Method" according to Eric Jaffe, *The King's Best Highway: Lost History of the Boston Post Road* (Scribner: New York, 2010), 132.

76 Harvey C. Mansfield and Delba Winthrop, trans. *Alexis de Tocqueville, Democracy in America* (Chicago: University of Chicago Press, 2000).

77 Hindley, *A History of Roads,* 85–87; Phil Patton, *Open Road: A Celebration of the American Highway* (New York: Simon & Schuster, 1986), 25.

78 Carol Sheriff, *The Artificial River: The Erie Canal and the Paradox of Progress, 1817–1862* (New York: Hill & Wang, 1996), 19-21.

79 Hindley, *A History of Roads,* 84–96.

80 Carlos Schwantes, *Going Places: Transportation Redefines the Twentieth Century West* (Bloomington: Indiana University Press, 2003), 6–39; According to Christian Wolmar, *The Great Railroad Revolution,* (New York: PublicAffairs, 2012), only 140,000 miles of track remain functional today, carrying 40 percent of the nation's freight.

81 Eric Jaffe, *The King's Best Highway,* 176–85.

82 Felix Rohatyn, *Bold Endeavors,* (New York: Simon & Schuster, 2009) 199–219

83 Hindley, *A History of Roads,* 110-112.

84 Exhibit: "Road Trip," California Archives, Secretary of State Building, Sacramento, CA, October 2007.

85 Patton, *Open Road*, 39-47; Schwantes, *Going Places*, 133-6.

86 Jaffe, *The King's Best Highway*, 194–200; Schwantes, *Going Places*, 152–5.

87 Arthur Krim, *Route 66: Iconography of the American Highway*, (Santa Fe,NM: Center Books on American Places, 2005).

88 Drake Hokanson, *The Lincoln Highway: Main Street Across America*, (Iowa City: University of Iowa Press, 1985), 58–64.; Schwantes, *Going Places*, 210–4.

89 Sources for legislation and building of the Interstate Highway System include: Phil Patton, *Open Road;* Felix Rohatyn, *Bold Endeavors;* Carlos Schwantes, *Going Places;* Tom Lewis, *Divided Highways: Building Interstate Highways; Transforming American Life*, (New York: Viking, 1997); Jean Edward Smith, *Eisenhower in War and Peace* (New York: Random House, 2012); Earl Swift, *The Big Roads* (New York: Houghton Mifflin Harcourt, 2011).

90 Smith, *Eisenhower in War and Peace*, 653.

91 For an elaboration of Mumford's critique of the interstate network, see Tom Lewis, *Divided Highways*.

Chapter 6 "Don't Tell Us About Snow!"

92 Chip Van Nattan interviewed in 2008 .

93 Senate Joint Resolution 89, June 29, 1965: DWP to Study Feasibility Including FH 100 in State Highway and Interstate System, by J. A. Cobey.

94 Position of USFS and NPS discussed during my interviews of Norman B. Livermore; Walter J. Puhn to N. B. Livermore, Jan. 26, 1966.

95 J. C. Womack, State Highway Engineer, "Study of Feasibility of Including FH100 in the State Highway System and The Interstate System a trans-Sierra Highway from Interstate 5 near Los Banos to California-Nevada State Line near Benton Station." Issued by California Department of Public Works, March 4, 1966.

96 At the time of its fiftieth anniversary in 2006, the National Interstate and Defense Highways Act actually provided for 47,876 miles of eligible thoroughfare; regarding traffic density studies, whether any utilization projections were meaningful is open to

question. Traffic on all interstates today is beyond the imagination of anyone when the network was first conceived.

97 *Bridgeport Chronicle-Union*, March 25, 1966; *Fresno Bee*, March 16, 1966.

98 *Fresno Bee*, March 26, 1966.

99 *Fresno Bee*, April 10, 1966,

100 FH 100 out of North Fork in the western foothills has become a National Scenic Byway, carries the number FH 81, and is still not fully paved. Minaret Summit Road down to the Devil's Postpile National Monument and Reds Meadow retains a single lane with pullouts to allow for two-way traffic.

101 Bob Tanner had previously served as athletic director for Bishop Union High School, and later as vice principal of the Home Street Middle School in Bishop, CA.

102 Lou Roeser interviewed 2009–2011; "Bid To Include Proposed Minaret Highway In State System is Killed," *Sacramento Bee*, April 19, 1967.

Chapter 7, Acts of Civil Disobedience

103 Members of this group of vandals were pleased to relate details of their misdeed to the author but asked for their longstanding anonymity to be honored.

104 N. B. Livermore to Judge Ray Sherwin, May 3, 1967; Judge Ray Sherwin to Genny Smith, June 28, 1967.

105 N. B. Livermore to John Erreca, July 25, 1967; John Erreca to. N. B. Livermore, Aug. 4 1967.

106 Pete Wilson to Douglas Kittredge, July 13, 1967.

107 Judge Ray Sherwin to Eric Van Nattan, May 10, 1967; Judge Ray Sherwin to Kent P. Connaughton, June 5, 1967.

108 N. B. Livermore to Fred L. Jones, August 2, 1967; Fred L. Jones to N. B. Livermore, August 14, 1967.

109 Story related during interviews of Mr. Livermore; also refer to "Man in the Middle"; "Sisk Charges Plot to Block Sierra Route," *Fresno Bee*, July 12, 1967.

110 "Livermore Denies Conflict," *Fresno Bee*, July 26, 1967.

111 George Skelton, "Sierra Road Called Folly," *Sacramento Union*, September 18, 1967.

112 "Livermore in the Eastern Sierra; Terms Idea 'Ludicrous and Cockeyed Road'," *Fresno Bee*, September 18, 1967.

113 N. B. Livermore to A. G. Mahan, October 26, 1967; County of Mono Resolution 37-67, Oct. 3, 1967; County of Inyo Resolution 67-104, November 6, 1967; County of Tuolumne Resolution 69-67: County of Mono Resolution 47-67, November 9, 1967.

114 S.B. 21 Recommending Acceptance into State Highway System CA 203 from Minaret Road in Mono County to Madera County at Minaret Summit, October 5, 1967 (see 203 file at Caltrans Library).

115 Ansel Adams to N. B. Livermore, February 18, 1968.

116 Assembly Bill 1191 introduced by Assemblymen Mobley and Zenovich, March 26, 1968, "An Act to Amend Section 503 of the Streets and Highway Code, relating to State Highway Route 203."

117 "Mobley Will Present Minarets Road Bill," *Fresno Bee*, March 26, 1968; N. B. Livermore, Statement from the Resources Agency of California, March 27, 1968.

118 Samuel B. Nelson to N. B. Livermore, April 2, 1968.

119 Bill Analysis for Department of Public Works, A.B. 1197, April 9, 1968.

120 Herbert Joseph MD, chairman, California Council for Trout Unlimited to Transportation Committee.

121 Charles W. Bonner to N. B. Livermore, April 24, 1968.

122 Bob Schotz interviewed several times.

123 N. B. Livermore, Statement For Presentation to the Assembly Transportation Committee Hearing, April 30, 1968.

124 A.B. 1191, Taken from the "Grid," California State Library (Legal Division). March 26, 1968.

125 "Committee to Take Up Minarets Road Bill," *Fresno Bee*, May 12, 1968.

126 "Solons Defer Mobley Bill and Minaret Summit Highway," *Fresno Bee*, May 15, 1968.

127 Judge Ray Sherwin memorandum to members, John Muir Trail Association, May 22, 1968.

128 Assemblyman Eugene Chappie, House Resolution 310 "Relative to the Minaret Summit Route," *Assembly Journal*, June 20, 1968.

129 Minutes of the Save the John Muir Trail Association for November 17, 1970; Marilyn Hayden to Judge Ray Sherwin (in which evidence of surveying activity is reported), November 15, 1970.

Chapter 8, Man in a White Hat

130 George Skelton, "The Man in the White Hat Who Saved the Sierra," *Los Angeles Times*, July 28, 1997; Jean Tanner, who was there, remembers a silver gray hat. It was James Watt who had embarrassed the Reagan Administration when in September 1983, he publically characterized his recently appointed Coal Commission with these ill-chosen words: "I have every kind of mixture you can have. I have a black, I have a woman, two Jews, and a cripple. We have talent." His resignation was accepted shortly thereafter. "Watt's Remark on Coal Panel Offends 4 Groups," *New York Times*, September 22, 1983, A15.

131 For context, the preceding sentence read, "I think too, that we've got to recognize that where the preservation of a resource like the redwoods is concerned, there is a common sense limit." Cited by Lou Cannon, *Governor Reagan: His Rise to Power*, (PublicAffairs, New York, 2003), 177.

132 Lou Cannon, *Governor Reagan*, 297–301.

133 1985 interview cited by Lou Cannon in *President Reagan: The Role of a Lifetime* (New York: PublicAffairs, 2000), 465. During his two-term presidency, he spent 345 days, nearly a full year, at Rancho del Cielo.

134 "Man in the Middle," 87.

135 *San Francisco Chronicle*, February 10, 1969.

136 Lou Cannon, *Governor Reagan: His Rise to Power*, 300–301.

137 According to Reagan biographer Lou Cannon, the Yukis preferred to be called Indians rather than Native Americans; Sacramento meeting is cited by Ted Simon, *The River Stops Here: Saving Round Valley, A Pivotal Chapter in California's Water Wars* (Berkeley: University of California Press, 1994) 314; Governor Reagan might have lost his Resources secretary at this point in their political collaboration when offers from Washington were considered but declined. Livermore preferred the job

he had rather than serve as undersecretary of the Interior (*Los Angeles Times,* February 22, 1970).

138 Cited by Cannon, *Governor Reagan,* 305.

139 N. B. Livermore, "Man in the Middle."

140 Letter from N. B. Livermore to D. R. Leisz, February 11, 1972; For Livermore reflection on challenge of bringing Reagan cabinet around to his thinking, refer to "Man in the Middle," 90.

141 Letter from Bob Tanner to N. B. Livermore, February 22, 1972; Secretary of Transportation John Volpe informed Governor Reagan that the gondola idea after review by the USFS was declared "unsuitable on aesthetic and economic grounds." Letter from Volpe to Reagan, June 8,1972.

142 Letter to John Volpe from Bob Kahn, member, Council on Environmental Quality, Executive Office of the President, April 24, 1972.

143 "Devil's Post Pile Road Work Funds Approved," *Bridgeport Chronicle-Union,* April 20, 1972.

144 Letters from Governor Ronald Reagan to secretary John Volpe, April 28 and May 30, 1972; letter from John Volpe to Ronald Reagan, June 8, 1972.

145 Letter from executive assistant Edwin Meese to secretary John A. Volpe, June 14, 1972; "Official State of California Comments On EIS For Forest Highway 100 to Minarets Summit," June 13, 1972.

146 "Nixon and Reagan: The California Boys," in Nancy Gibbs and Michael Duffy, *The President's Club* (New York: Simon & Schuster, 2012), 191–257.

147 Memorandum with attachments, OMB director Caspar Weinberger to presidential assistant John Ehrlichman, June 22, 1972.

148 Carl Bernstein and Bob Woodward, *All the President's Men,* (New York: Simon & Schuster, 1974); Nixon quote on page 29.

149 Lou Cannon, *Governor Reagan,* 318.

150 Jean Tanner interviewed in 2012 and 2014.

151 Interviews of Lou and Marye Roesser, 2008–2012.

152 Dignitaries joining the party included assistant secretary of the Interior John W. Larson; James Stearns, state director of Conservation; Ford B. Ford, deputy secretary for Resources;

state senator Howard Way; assemblyman Gene Chappie; and Edgar Wayburn representing the Sierra Club.

153 In 1972, the California governor's security was provided by the California State Police, later absorbed by the California Highway Patrol in 1995.

154 Entire conversation vividly recalled by Jean Tanner.

155 Spider K, Jean Tanner reminds, performed in thirty Rose Bowl Parades!

156 For trail information refer to Genny Smith, *Mammoth Lakes Sierra; A Handbook for Roadside and Trail,* (Mammoth Lakes: Genny Smith Books, Seventh Edition, 2003).

157 Pumice: a geologic term for volcanic rock, formed from frothy lava, famous for floating on water.

158 Sheep herding, common in the Sierra around 1900 came to an end when the US Army was commissioned to drive the herds down into the Sierra Foothills at the urging of John Muir.

159 Full text of telegram: "The President announced today that the proposed reconstruction of a portion of the Minarets Highway in California will not be undertaken. And the proposed Trans-Sierra Highway (Forest Highway 100) will not be built. The President said he agreed with the recommendations of Governor Reagan of California that damage would be done to the environment by the reconstruction of a portion of the existing highway, and by the construction of long proposed Trans-Sierra Highway. The President said the environmental considerations and the need to preserve the atmosphere and ecology of the Sierra region of California clearly overrode the other factors that had been urged in supporting the construction proposals."

160 In the absence of Secretary Volpe, his deputy James Beggs offered, "reluctant agreement with the president's decision," according to Weinberger. The 2.7-mile road segment was eventually paved in 1978, with budgeted forest highway improvement funds that required no special appropriation bill. This limited the scope of the project. The extensive cuts required for a two-lane road, first surveyed years before, have never been made.

161 "Trans-Sierra Road Project Called Off," *Los Angeles Times,* June 29, 1972; "Media Cover Statement by Governor," *Inyo*

Register, July 6, 1972; "Governor Reagan Takes to the Saddle," *Fresno Bee,* June 29, 1972

162 Cannon, *Governor Reagan,* 321.

Chapter 9, The Idea of a Managed Wilderness

163 Roderick Frazier Nash, *Wilderness and the American Mind* (New Haven, CT: Yale University Press, 1967), xi.

164 Robert Marshall, "The Problem of a Wilderness," *Scientific Monthly,* 30 (1930), 141; Aldo Leopold, "The Wilderness and its Place in Forest Recreational Policy," *Journal of Forestry,* 19 (1921), 719.

165 US, *Statutes at Large,* 78. 891.

166 Refer to Deuteronomy, chapters 8 and 16; Isaiah, chapters 35 and 42.

167 William Bradford cited by Nash, *Wilderness and the American Mind,* 24.

168 Chief Standing Bear cited by Nash, *Wilderness and the American Mind,* xiii.

169 Alexis de Tocqueville, *Democracy in America,* edited by Phillips Bradley, (New York: Vintage Books, 1945), 2, 74.

170 Charles Fenno Hoffman, *American Monthly Magazine,* 8 (1836) 469: Charles Lanman, *A Summer in the Wilderness* (New York: D. Appleton & Company, 1847) 105.

171 Fremont's description cited by Francis P. Farquhar, *History of the Sierra Nevada* (Berkeley: University of California Press,1965), 62. Farquhar places Fremont and his party on modern day Red Lake Peak near US 50.

172 See Walter Harding, "A Checklist of Thoreau's Lectures," *Bulletin of the New York Public Library,* 52 (1948) 82.

173 From Thoreau's Walden, *Writings of Henry David Thoreau,* cited by Nash, *Wilderness in the American Mind,* 92.

174 Francis Parkman in 1892 edition of *The Oregon Trail,* cited by Nash, *Wilderness and the American Mind,* 100.

175 John Ise, *Our National Park Policy: A Critical History,* (Baltimore: Johns Hopkins University Press, 1961), 13; Frederick Law Olmstead Papers, Library of Congress, cited by Nash, *Wilderness and the American Mind,* 106.

176 Cited by Nash, *Wilderness and the American Mind*, 161.

177 As documented by the *National Geographic* and reported on the Theodore Roosevelt Association website: www.theodore-roosevelt.org/life/conservation. The list includes 150 national forests, 51 federal bird reservations, 4 national game preserves, 5 national parks, 18 national monuments, and 24 reclamation projects.

178 Cited by Nash, *Wilderness and the American Mind*, 161.

179 Ibid., 134-138.

180 Char Miller, *Gifford Pinchot and the Making of Modern Environmentalism*, (Washington, DC: Island Press/Shearwater Books, 2001).

181 S. 1176 introduced in the US Senate on February 11, 1957 (also printed in *Living Wilderness*, 21, 1956-1957, 26-36).

182 David Brower in Senate Hearings, cited by Nash, *Wilderness and the American Mind*, 225.

183 Michael McCloskey, "The Wilderness Act of 1964: Its Background and Meaning," *Oregon Law Review*, 45 (1966) 288-321.

184 Nash, *Wilderness and the American Mind*, 379.

Chapter 10, Stopping the Road

185 Ronald Reagan to Alan Cranston, August 8, 1972.

186 Genny Smith to Lou Roeser, May 18, 1972.

187 Ronald Reagan to Ray Sherwin, June 13, 1972; Ronald Reagan to Mrs. Ward C. Smith, July 24, 1972.

188 B. F. Sisk to Ronald Reagan, August 17, 1972.

189 Governor Ronald Reagan to Rep. B. F. Sisk, November 22, 1972.

190 "3 Mile Road Improvement Reported," *Fresno Bee*, November 4, 1975.

191 Genny Smith to Ray Sherwin, January 23, 1976.

192 "Nevada Senate Beats Drums for Minaret Road," *Fresno Bee*, January 7, 1973.

193 N. B. Livermore to Mrs. Ward C. Smith, March 14, 1973.

194 Zane G. Smith to Anthony J. Chasteen, March 19, 1970 (traces derivation of use of San Joaquin Wilderness in the naming of a prospective wilderness area and an advocacy organization.

195 N. B. Livermore to Hal Thomas, January 15, 1979; advisory board included Ray Sherwin, Mammoth Lakes; Genny Smith, Palo Alto; George Whitmore, Fresno; Hal Thomas, Clovis; Gary Schroeder, Fresno; Margaret Molarsky, Ross; Tony Chasteen, Sebastapol; John Modin, El Dorado Hills; Lynne Foster, Mammoth Lakes; Norman B. Livermore, San Rafael; Beverly Steveson, Bakersfield; Cynthia Connolly, Fresno; Martin Litton, Portola Valley; and August Fruge, Berkeley.

196 "House Approves $1.3 Billion Bill to Expand Park," *Wall Street Journal*, July 13, 1978; "Carter Signs Endangered American Wilderness Act," *Newsletter of the Wilderness Society*, February 2, 1978; National Wilderness Fact Sheet, Genny Smith Papers, Bancroft Library, UC–Berkeley.

197 RARE is a function of government that continues. As of 1998, there were 60 million acres of land inventoried, 9 million in Idaho, which is the state with the most roadless lands, presumably available for wilderness designation.

198 N. B. Livermore to Zane Gray Smith, regional forester, September 28, 1978; Ray Sherwin to Hal Thomas, November 21, 1978; N. B. Livermore to Hal Thomas, January 15, 1979; Hal Thomas to Ray Sherwin, January 15, 1979.

199 Genny Smith to Robert L. Rice, superintendent Inyo National Forest, September 12, 1978; Genny Smith to Ed Baltz, FWSA, April 21, 1979.

200 Genny Smith to Ira Hanson, February 22, 1980; According to Mammoth Mountain Winter Recreation Masterplan Alternatives, July 1978, preliminary planning for backside development included eight new lifts and 582 acres of trails.

201 Gary H. McCoy to John Seiberling, March 26, 1980; John F. Seiberling to Gary H. McCoy, April 15, 1980; Noteworthy is the fact that expansion into any of these areas has not taken place, owing to a changing winter recreation demography.

202 Harold Thomas to congressman Phillip Burton, March 5, 1979.

203 Genny Smith to Harold Thomas, March 13, 1979.

204 John Modin, statement on behalf of San Joaquin Wilderness Association, October 6, 1979; For H.R. 859 history, refer to http://www.environs.law,ucdavis.edu.

205 Genny Smith, testimony for H.R. 859 hearing, Washington DC, June 18, 1981, Genny Smith Papers, Bancroft Library, UC–Berkeley.

206 An amoeba is one of the simplest living organisms, a protozoan, whose shape constantly changes because of the projection of its pseudopods (false feet).

207 Russ Shay, Sierra Club bulletin announcing death of congressman Phil Burton, April 19, 1983.

208 Phillip Burton, H.R. 1437, "California Wilderness Act of 1983" introd uced February 15, 1983.

209 Escape for Mammoth Lakes residents was escape from seismic threats; the city sits on the edge of one of the continent's largest calderas with visible geothermal zones and frequent tremblors.

210 Alan Cranston, "Memorandum: Status of Senate Bill 5 (H.R. 1437; "Burton Bill") regarding wilderness areas, May 19, 1983.

211 *Fresno Bee*, July 5, 1984; "Senator Wilson's New Position," *Sierra Club Bulletin*, February 10, 1984; *Fresno Bee*, July 11, 1984.

212 *Fresno Bee*, July 7, 1984.

213 Term coined by Elbridge Gerry to describe the redefinition of boundaries for election districts in order to influence outcomes. Gerry likened the outcome to a salamander regrowing its amputated limbs, thus "to gerrymander."

214 Public Law 98-425: An Act Entitled: California Wilderness Act of 1984 (H.R. 1437), Sept. 28, 1984; in subsequent accountings of Ronald Reagan's environmental record, both as governor and as president, the California Wilderness Act of 1984 was not listed.

215 Genny Smith to N. B. Livermore, May 14, 1985; N. B. Livermore to Genny Smith, May 23, 1985; Color printing was off budget for the SJWA and so for maps fashioned to display the prospective designated area, Genny sat for hours with her color pencils applying key colors to each copy. Former Mono County Supervisor Andrea Lawrence recalled a comment made by Genny's geologist husband Ward Smith: "I regret that I have but one wife to give to my nation."

216 Ansel Adams to N. B. Livermore, February 18, 1968; His entire sentence read, "I honestly believe that as the Minaret Summit

is the least important and least interesting pass of the Sierra south of Sonora Pass, that a road in this area would do the least possible damage." He went on to suggest that, "We lost Tioga because this Minaret Summit Road was not in existence."

217 *Congressional Quarterly Almanac,* 98th Congress 2nd Session, 1984, Vol. XL, 315.

218 N. B. Livermore to Sally Rakov, state director for senator Pete Wilson, May 25, 1983.

Chapter 11, "We Were Lucky"

219 Quotes taken from Genny Smith's recollections titled, "Some Personal Comments" as well as from her speech, "Political Strategy – The Ansel Adams Wilderness," delivered to the Mono Lake Committee on July 26, 1985.

220 Robert Schneider to Genny Smith, May 2, 1967.

221 An attempt to establish a link between politics in 1972 and higher-level maneuvering in 1984 proved unsuccessful. Each campaign was influenced by prevailing circumstances of the moment.

222 Judge Sherwin, a 1979 victim of cancer, did not live to see final resolution of the road issue.

Epilogue

223 "Snow Removal Operations on I-80," California Department of Transportaion, District 3, 2002; Report provided by Stanley Richins, District 3 regional manager.

224 Averaged over the span of a year, commercial goods valued at one to two million dollars passes over Donner Pass every hour of the day.

225 Gene Rose, *High Odyssey* (Fresno, CA: Panorama West Books, 1987); avalanche control efforts are limited to multiple use areas; e.g. ski areas and high-altitude canyons through which highways pass, but they prevail throughout mountain ranges wherever snow accumulates on inclined surfaces.

BIBLIOGRAPHY

Bernstein, Carl, and Bob Woodward. *All the President's Men*. New York: Simon & Schuster, 1974.

"Bid To Include Proposed Minaret Highway In State System is Killed." *Sacramento Bee*, April 19, 1967.

Caldwell, Gary. *Mammoth Gold: The Ghost Towns of Lake District*. Mammoth Lakes, CA: Genny Smith Books, 1990.

Cannon, Lou. *Governor Reagan: His Rise to Power*. New York: PublicAffairs, 2003.

"Carter Signs Endangered American Wilderness Act." *Newsletter of the Wilderness Society*, February 2, 1978.

Chappie, Eugene. "Relative to the Minaret Summit Route." House Resolution 310. *Assembly Journal*, June 20, 1968.

"Committee to Take Up Minarets Road Bill." *Fresno Bee*, May 12, 1968.

"Congressman B.F. Sisk Asks for Speed-up of Route Studies." *Fresno Bee*, November 18, 1964.

de Tocqueville, Alexis. *Democracy in America*. Edited by Phillips Bradley. New York: Vintage Books, 1945.

"Devil's Post Pile Road Work Funds Approved." *Bridgeport Chronicle-Union*, April 20, 1972.

Farquhar, Francis P. *History of the Sierra Nevada*. Berkeley: University of California Press, 1965.

"FCC Seeks All Year Sierra Road." *Fresno Bee*, December 16, 1959.

Fey, Marshall, R. Joe King, and Jack Lepisto. *Emigrant Shadows: A History and Guide to the California Trail*. Virginia City, NV: Western Trails Research Association, 2002.

Frazier, Ian. "Travels in Siberia: The Ultimate Road Trip." *New Yorker*, August 3, 2009.

Gibbs, Nancy, and Michael Duffy. *The President's Club*. New York: Simon & Schuster, 2012.

"Governor Reagan Takes to the Saddle." *Fresno Bee*, June 29, 1972.

Harding, Walter. "A Checklist of Thoreau's Lectures." *Bulletin of the New York Public Library*, 52 (1948): 82.

Heizer, R. F., and M. A. Whipple. *The California Indians: A Source Book*. Berkeley: University of California Press, 1971.

"Highway Over Sierra Sought As Defense Project." *Fresno Bee*, August 24, 1941.

Hill, Mary. *Geology of the Sierra Nevada*. Berkeley: University of California Press, 2006.

Hindley, Geoffrey. *A History of Roads*. London: Peter Davies, 1971.

Hoffman, Charles Fenno. *American Monthly Magazine*, 8 (1836): 469.

Hokanson, Drake. *The Lincoln Highway: Main Street Across America*. Iowa City: University of Iowa Press, 1985.

"House Approves $1.3 Billion Bill to Expand Park." *Wall Street Journal*, July 13, 1978.

Howard, Thomas Frederick. *Sierra Crossing: First Roads to California*. Berkeley: University of California Press, 1998.

"Improvements to the Eastern End of Tioga Pass Road." News Release, State of California Department of Public Works. February 9, 1966 for publication in *California Highways and Public Works Magazine*, January-February 1966.

Ise, John. *Our National Park Policy: A Critical History*. Baltimore, MD: Johns Hopkins University Press, 1961.

Jaffe, Eric. *The King's Best Highway: Lost History of the Boston Post Road*. New York: Scribner: 2010.

"Justice Douglas Opposes Highway." *Fresno Bee*. September 15, 1959.

Krim, Arthur. *Route 66: Iconography of the American Highway*. Santa Fe, NM: Center Books on American Places, 2005.

Lanman, Charles. *A Summer in the Wilderness*. New York: D. Appleton & Company, 1847.

Leopold, Aldo. "The Wilderness and its Place in Forest Recreational Policy" *Journal of Forestry* 19 (1921): 719.

Lewis, Tom. *Divided Highways: Building Interstate Highways; Transforming American Life*. New York: Viking, 1997.

"Livermore Denies Conflict." *Fresno Bee*, July 26, 1967.

"Livermore in the Eastern Sierra; Terms Idea 'Ludicrous and Cockeyed Road.' " *Fresno Bee*, September 18, 1967.

Livermore, Norman B., Jr. "Packing in 50 Years Ago." In *The Album: Times and Tales of Inyo-Mono County*, Bishop, CA: Chalfant Press, 1990.

Livermore, Norman B., Jr. "Roads Running Wild," *American Forests,* April 1938.

"Maderans Back Northfork to Nevada Route." *Fresno Bee,* February 19, 1939.

Mansfield, Harvey C., and Delba Winthrop, trans. *Alexis de Tocqueville, Democracy in America,* Chicago: University of Chicago Press, 2000.

Marshall, Robert. "The Problem of a Wilderness." *Scientific Monthly* 30 (1930): 141.

McCloskey, Michael. "The Wilderness Act of 1964: Its Background and Meaning." *Oregon Law Review* 45 (1966): 288–321.

McGlashan, Charles F. *History of the Donner Party: A Tragedy of the Sierra.* New York: Barnes & Noble, 2004.

McPhee, John. *Assembling California.* New York: Farrar, Straus, and Giroux, 1993.

"Media Cover Statement by Governor" *Inyo Register,* July 6, 1972.

Miller, Char. *Gifford Pinchot and the Making of Modern Environmentalism.* Washington, DC: Island Press/Shearwater Books, 2001.

"Millions of Acres Win Wilderness Protection." *Congressional Quarterly Almanac 1984.* Washington, DC: Congressional Quarterly, 1985.

"Mobley Will Present Minarets Road Bill." *Fresno Bee,* March 26, 1968.

Morning, Robin. *Tracks of Passion: Eastern Sierra Skiing, Dave McCoy, and Mammoth Mountain.* Mammoth Lakes, CA: Mammoth Lakes Foundation, 2008.

Nash, Roderick Frazier. *Wilderness and the American Mind.* New Haven, CT: Yale University Press, 1967.

"Nevada Senate Beats Drums for Minaret Road." *Fresno Bee,* January 7, 1973.

Patera, Alan H. *Bennettville and the Tioga Mining District.* Western Places Monograph Series. Lake Grove, OR: Western Places, 2003.

Patton, Phil. *Open Road: A Celebration of the American Highway.* New York: Simon & Schuster, 1986.

"Opponents of Mammoth Road Name Officers." *Fresno Bee,* July 23, 1957.

Reed, Adele. *Old Mammoth*. Palo Alto, CA: Genny Smith Books, 1982.

"Road is Needed." *Fresno Bee*, June 18, 1946.

"Roads to Somewhere: The Highways that Have Changed America's Social and Economic Face." *The Economist*, June 24, 2006.

Rohatyn, Felix. *Bold Endeavors*. New York: Simon & Schuster, 2009.

Rose, Gene. *High Odyssey*. Fresno, CA: Panorama West Books, 1987.

Schwantes, Carlos. *Going Places: Transportation Redefines the Twentieth Century West*. Bloomington: Indiana University Press, 2003.

"Senator Wilson's New Position." *Sierra Club Bulletin*, February 10, 1984.

Sheriff, Carol. *The Artificial River: The Erie Canal and the Paradox of Progress, 1817–1862*. New York: Hill & Wang, 1996.

Sherwin, Ray. "Mammoth Pass Road Newsletter," February 21, 1963.

Sherwin, Ray. "Minaret Summit to North Fork: Wilderness or Trans-Sierra Highway," 1966.

"Sierra Club Reaffirms Stand Against MPR." *Fresno Bee*, September 29, 1959.

Simon, Ted. *The River Stops Here: Saving Round Valley, A Pivotal Chapter in California's Water Wars*. Berkeley: University of California Press, 1994.

"Sisk Backs Road to Link Rockies With Valley." *Fresno Bee*, April 25, 1965.

"Sisk Charges Plot to Block Sierra Route." *Fresno Bee*, July 12, 1967.

Skelton, George. "The Man in the White Hat Who Saved the Sierra." *Los Angeles Times*, July 28, 1997

Skelton, George. "Sierra Road Called Folly," *Sacramento Union*, September 18, 1967.

Smith, Genny. *Mammoth Lakes Sierra; A Handbook for Roadside and Trail*. 7th ed. Mammoth Lakes, CA: Genny Smith Books, 2003.

Smith, Jean Edward. *Eisenhower in War and Peace*. New York: Random House, 2012.

"Solons Defer Mobley Bill and Minaret Summit Highway." *Fresno Bee,* May 15, 1968.

Starr, Kevin. *California: A History.* New York: Modern Library, 2005.

"Supervisors See Need to Extend Mammoth Road." *Fresno Bee,* August 15, 1953.

Swift, Earl. *The Big Roads.* New York: Houghton Mifflin Harcourt, 2011.

"3 Mile Road Improvement Reported." *Fresno Bee,* November 4, 1975.

"Trans-Sierra Highway Plan Said Feasible." *Bakersfield Californian,* November 19, 1958.

"Trans-Sierra Road Project Called Off." *Los Angeles Times,* June 29, 1972.

Van Nattan, W. E. "Why Should There Be A Mammoth Pass Road?" Fact sheet, Mono County Resources Committee, Mammoth Lakes, CA, 1968.

"Watt's Remark on Coal Panel Offends 4 Groups." *New York Times,* September 22, 1983.

White, Richard. *Railroaded: The Transcontinentals and the Making of Modern America.* New York: W. W. Norton, 2011.

Wolmar, Christian. *The Great Railroad Revolution.* New York: PublicAffairs, 2012.

ART CREDITS

MAPS COURTESY OF California Dept. of Transportation, copyright 1965.

Photographs of Ike Livermore provided by his son, David Livermore, and by Phil Pister.

Photographs of themselves provided by Genny Smith, Bob and Peggy Schotz, Lou and Marye Roeser, Jean Tanner.

Photographs of Governor Reagan at Reds Meadow Pack Station and Summit Meadow taken by her late husband, Russ Johnson, courtesy of Anne Johnson.

Sierra Landscapes provided by Nature Photographer Steve Ingram, Swall Meadows, CA. www.ingramphoto.com.

ACKNOWLEDGMENTS

FIRST HONORS GO to Bob Schotz for directing me to this story. "So many books on the water wars," he grumbled. "Nobody has written about us stopping that road from coming through here." With his guidance, I soon found many of the "road warriors," all of them willing to recall their experiences. Plenty of documentary evidence awaited me as well.

Norman Livermore welcomed me into his San Rafael home. "Just call me Ike," was his opening line. Wife Dina soon joined us and offered her perspective. For Ike, integrity of the John Muir Trail meant everything, and he was thrilled by the prospect of a book about the victory. Since his passing, I have been faithfully assisted by his son David.

Judge Ray Sherwin was no longer available for interview, yet deserves posthumous recognition for the abundance of his written product on the road issue: published summaries, judicial briefs, correspondence, and especially the diaries from walking every mile of the problematic corridor zone.

Genny Smith, whose comprehensive guidebooks I had long depended on, invited me first to her home in Cupertino, and later to her Sierra cabin tucked between Mineral Ridge and Mammoth Mountain. Although her papers are held at the Bancroft Library in Berkeley, she retained an excellent sampling of copies for our mutual study. She has stood by me all the way, keeping me honest with respect to both geography and geology. "There are no Sierra Mountains," she reminded me. "It is the Sierra Nevada plain and simple!" And: "While you are correct that granite dominates the ridge above Devils Postpile, remember there is a lot of metamorphic rock there too."

Marye and Lou Roeser recalled so many events from the lengthy battle. Bob Tanner, until recently operator of Reds Meadow Pack Station, remains a fascinating raconteur of local history. Also available to me were Dorothy and Lou Fitzhugh, Marilyn Hayden,

Andrea Lawrence, Dave McCoy and his son Gary, Lee Roeser, Peggy Schotz, Chip Van Nattan, Lynda and Lloyd Wilson. Hostess for the Reagan wilderness ride, Jean Tanner, remembers everything including her spat with the governor's security detail.

Everyone who writes about the past knows the value of libraries and archivists. I was capably served by the California State Library, Theresa Salazar and her staff at the Bancroft Library, Jason Schultz at the Richard Nixon Presidential Library, Barbara Moss at the Laws Railroad Museum, and especially Deborah Cismowski at the remarkable Caltrans Transportation Library and History Center. Most numbered highways in California enjoy their very own historical file. Caltrans Region 3 Manager Stan Richins explained for me how I-80 is kept open during a winter storm.

Essential reviewers of the manuscript include Phil Pister, formerly of California Fish and Wildlife; Chris Johnson, National Park Service historian, Bob Pavlik, Caltrans Environmental Planner and Historian, and Richard Mallard, fellow Eastern Sierra historian. Deanna Dulen, Superintendent of Devils Postpile National Monument, has been enthusiastic for the project from the outset.

For the book itself, I thank first, writer/editor/publisher Mike Sager for timely suggestions that produced an improved story line, and second, The Sager Group whose many talented collaborators include designer Siori Kitajima for design, copyeditor Jean McDonald, and programmers Ovidiu Vlad and Andreea Vlad. Peggy Schotz, whose Mammoth Sierra watercolors are widely regarded, generously offered the cover art. Steve Ingram, nature photographer, provided additional art. And how fortunate can a writer be to have available cousin Carol Bunce's spectacular Rocking K Ranch in Bishop and the idyllic home of Pat and Dale Gilbert for use in Mammoth Lakes?

ABOUT THE AUTHOR

JACK FISHER IS a physician and professor emeritus of surgery at U.C. San Diego. After twenty years as head of the division of plastic and reconstructive surgery, he retired and earned a master's degree in U.S. political and economic history. Stopping the Road is his third narrative history, a labor of love for California's Eastern Sierra.

ABOUT THE PUBLISHER

THE SAGER GROUP was founded in 1984. In 2012 it was chartered as a multi-media artists' and writers' consortium, with the intent of empowering those who make art—an umbrella beneath which makers can pursue, and profit from, their craft directly, without gatekeepers. TSG publishes eBooks and paper books; manages musical acts and produces live shows; ministers to artists and provides modest grants; and produces documentary, feature and web-based films. By harnessing the means of production, The Sager Group helps artists help themselves. For more information, please see www.TheSagerGroup.Net.